1940

1940

The Story of No. 11 Group, Fighter Command

by

Peter G. Cooksley

ROBERT HALE · LONDON

First published in Great Britain 1983
© *1983 Peter G. Cooksley*

ISBN 0 7090 0907 0

Robert Hale Limited
Clerkenwell House
Clerkenwell Green
London EC1R 0HT

Photoset in Palatino by
Kelly Typesetting Limited
Bradford-on-Avon, Wiltshire
Printed in Great Britain by
St Edmundsbury Press
Bury St Edmunds, Suffolk
Bound by Woolnough Bookbinding Limited, Northants

Contents

List of Illustrations

Between pages 96 and 97

Hugh Dowding, AOC-in-C of Fighter Command in 1940
   (*Imperial War Museum*)
Keith Park, the brilliant tactician in charge of 11 Group
Badge of No. 11 Group, Fighter Command
Pilots of No. 19 Squadron (*Crown Copyright Reserved*)
Barrage balloon in Victoria Embankment Gardens (*IPC
   Transport Press*)
The same site as it appeared in 1981
Vapour trails mark the progress of a battle
Junkers 87s dive-bomb a Channel convoy on 14th July
   (*Imperial War Museum*)
Dover Harbour under attack
A Spitfire of No. 65 Squadron being refuelled (*IPC Transport
   Press*)

8   *List of Illustrations*

Acknowledgements

A wide range of research facilities, libraries, agencies, archives and individuals were consulted before this book was written, either to gather accurate information or in the search for photographs; foremost of all these are the following, to whom sincere thanks are extended:
K. A. Belcher; Dover Museum and Library; G. Fry; V. J. Garwood; Sir Gerald Gibbs, KBE, CIE, MC; IPC Transport Press; The Imperial War Museum; W. A. Jones; D. Knight; The Ministry of Defence (Air); The Public Record Office; D. B. Robertson; D. R. Samson; P. Ward-Smith.

Preface

There could be no more appropriate motto for the former Fighter Command's No. 11 Group than the one chosen which summed up its principal role, *Tutela Cordis*—"Defend the Heart", since in the midst of its area was the prime target of Britain's capital, London.

In the summer of 1940 this defence was fully put to the test, the result being in truth a modern David and Goliath encounter that was to rival any that folklore has to offer.

The seemingly insatiable interest in the struggle which became the Battle of Britain is at first difficult to explain, since the events of 1940 are now approaching half a century behind us. But it may be that the appeal is due to its placing each one of us in the midst of history, so to speak. There is little to mark the time when Napoleon cast envious eyes on the chalk cliffs at Dover, and even less that brings alive again the days in the reign of the first Queen Elizabeth when our island was threatened by an invader, yet every street and field in much of the corner of England that was 11 Group's fighting area will have witnessed the struggle for survival to which the only alternative was subjugation and death.

That this took place within the memories of many still in our midst has meant that the Battle of Britain has collected even now its own legends, all less astonishing than the truth. Perhaps the most persistent of these is that the saviours of Great Britain, and as the text makes clear, no doubt the United States as well, were a bunch of debonair and seemingly invincible young men who carried all before them and drove the Nazis from the skies of South-East England. Nothing could be further from the truth, and the survivors whose names have become famous agree with this, for the victory achieved in the skies of 1940 over No. 11 and its associated Groups was won by the pilots who came to a squadron and scored a few victories before themselves falling, frequently even before their names had become known to their colleagues. These and the lucky ones who lasted a little longer until weariness finally beat them were among the real victors.

Yet there were others, no less victorious: the ground-crews who kept the flyers aloft and toiled without the reward of public adulation. They filled the bomb-craters, excavated for the dead and tuned Merlin engines calmly while all hell reigned overhead; not for them the death in battle with the adrenalin flowing but often a miserable end in a trench or a slow and painful one riddled with splinters of bomb or glass. This book tells their stories too, and what they thought and did in 11 Group at that time.

Others who have received scant recognition are the senior officers who directed the meagre force of defenders, and something of these is also told here against the background of the history of Fighter Command's No. 11 Group as it bore the brunt of the assault that could end only with invasion.

PETER G. COOKSLEY
London, 1983

Part One

CHAPTER ONE

The Scene is Set

It was the twinkling lights as the evening sun danced on the canopies of the aircraft that first caught the boy's attention so that he paused, leaning on his bicycle, to take a better look at the eighteen gyrating shapes silhouetted against the backdrop of the summer sky; idly he looked at his watch, it was just before seven o'clock. Unknown to him there had been plenty of indications that the machines he was watching were hostile, for there had been considerable activity which up to that moment had not touched the comparative tranquillity of the civilian world although Britain had been at war with Nazi Germany for almost a year. His two surprised sisters, elsewhere in the district, had been advised to get indoors by a policeman who had emerged from the blue telephone box that stood a short distance from their home. In fact a "yellow" warning had been in operation since 6.29 p.m. but of this most people knew nothing.

Quite suddenly, the formation seemed to make up a collective mind and, still performing what another lad's mother was to describe as "acrobatics" as she watched from her son's bedroom window, the twin groups of nine two-engined machines swung in from the north and swooped down towards the local aerodrome, evasive action and a shallow dive taking them swiftly down from the 8,000 feet at which they had approached.

A short distance away the formation was also being watched by the pair manning Yolk 2, the local post of the Observer Corps, the body not yet enjoying "Royal" as part of its title. Bewildered by the lack of a civilian warning, the two men nevertheless had recognized the silhouettes on which they kept their glasses trained, but when several dark shapes dropped away from the first machines, surprise for a moment routed correct reporting procedures when one of the men blurted into the mouthpiece of the field telephone strapped about his chest, "They're bombing the aerodrome, Centre!" The Battle of Britain had come to the heart of Fighter Command's No. 11 Group.

Up until this time the immediate signs of a country at war had been as small as they were varied, although it was inescapable that the position was grave. Buses had their windows protected against anticipated blast by adhesive green netting, men and women walked the streets in boiler suits, not yet called "battledress", with the letters "ARP" on the front, and post-boxes had greenish-yellow tops from a coat of paint which would give visual warning of a poison-gas attack. The wireless, as most people still called radio, had kept listeners abreast of a deteriorating situation, for apart from this and the traditional newspaper no other form of mass communication existed since the new television, scarcely beyond its embryo stage had been suddenly closed down at the outbreak of war. Nevertheless its short pioneer life had made a considerable contribution to the battle about to be waged, as we shall see.

The previous winter had been one of the coldest which

could be remembered. A forty-five year record had been broken by the freezing weather that lasted, with only a single break, from the end of December until the middle of the following February. Conditions were such that trains were arriving at their destinations not hours but days late, while off the Dover coast the Strait froze solid at Folkestone and also at Dungeness. Inland too conditions showed no sign of improving. It was reported that eight miles of solid ice were blocking the River Thames between Sunbury and Teddington, although tales such as these could be passed on only by word of mouth since censorship approached the ridiculous, not for the first time, when references to the severity of the weather were forbidden.

It was not only Britain that shivered in the iron clasp of winter. The Continent of Europe suffered also, and in France where the new British Expeditionary Force strove to keep the oil in tank engines at least semi-liquid and BBC engineers took their recording discs to bed with them to prevent their splitting with the cold, burials had to be post-poned until the unyielding ground could be dug.

Poland, in defence of which Britain had gone to war, had already been erased from the map of Europe during an eighteen-day campaign that had ended when President Mościcki, Marshal Rydz-Smigly and Colonel Beck had fled with the rest of their government, although it was to be another ten days before Warsaw surrendered after a pro-longed resistance that was more foolish than heroic.

With the coming of spring the Wehrmacht was to leap into action again, not only on the Western Front, where constant propaganda assured all and sundry in both France and Britain that the permanent subterranean defences known as the Maginot Line were impenetrable, but also in Scandinavia. There, with a use of air power that was then unique, the Nazi hordes had struck at Denmark on 9th April 1940, the massive aerial attacks both from high and low level bringing all resistance to an almost bloodless halt. Neighbouring Norway too was on the receiving end of the

first real air invasion the world had seen when, based on
experience that had been digested during the winter
months after the attack on Poland, transport aircraft so
many in number that they seemed to darken the sky had
dropped men in such great numbers over Oslo that all
resistance was quickly suppressed among the harbours and
fjords.

In an attempt to reverse this alarming situation Britain
and France had sent land forces to northern and central
Norway while the landings were supported by aircraft
flying from vessels off Trondheim. All too soon the decision
was taken to withdraw and the same Naval units were
detailed to cover this operation at the beginning of June.
However, by this time there had tended to be other events
of more immediate importance to concern men's minds,
although the Scandinavian situation was still reported
along with events in Finland. There, until the collapse of all
resistance brought about an armistice on 13th March 1940,
Joseph Stalin's Soviet Union had been conducting a campaign since 30th November 1939.

What was increasingly occupying everyone at home,
both civilians and those in the services, was the situation in
France, the almost traditional battleground of Europe since
the days of Agincourt, Poitiers and Crécy nearly six
hundred years before. While the campaign in Norway was
still undecided, a Nazi offensive had been launched during
the early hours of 10th May 1940, and although the ultimate
target was certainly France the first waves of invaders were
thrown against the ill-defended German border with
Holland, ten Panzer divisions being put into the field with
627 new Pzkw III and IV tanks. The remainder of the total of
just under three thousand were earlier models usually
regarded as inferior to their Allied counterparts of which
there was a greater number although less well organized,
a fact that was to cost the British and French very dear
indeed.

The bitter fighting that ensued came to a head on that

day. By this time the motorized divisions of the Wehrmacht's 4th, 6th and part of the 12th Armies had rolled the
defence back to a line running southwards from Wavre to
north of Sedan, the sector south of Antwerp being in the
hands of Belgian troops.

Announcement of a Nazi breakthrough came with the
news that the defence along the Meuse at Maastricht had
collapsed, allowing two Panzer divisions and a motorized
division to penetrate as far as Wavre in an area that had
already seen several withdrawals which the media were
always careful to describe as "strategic" or "according to
plan".

To the north and south of this part of the Front the
situation was similarly grave, for part of the 12th Army's
Panzer Gruppe had penetrated the Allied positions north of
Carignan and was to sweep on across the Somme at St
Quentin and continue behind the Allied positions towards
Calais.

Meanwhile the advancing 18th Army was to break
through near Breda and swing northwards to Rotterdam,
where support was to come from concentrated paratroop
landings over a wide area. This too was a new form of
attack, for although much publicity had been given to the
preparation of similar forces within the Soviet Union, their
appearance in France opened a fresh chapter in modern
warfare. So did the use of a comparatively small number of
gliders to enable troops to silence the defenders of the
Belgian Eben-Emael fortress and to take the vital bridges
over the Albert Canal that would otherwise have been
defended to slow the Nazi advance.

It was only four days later that a determined attempt was
made to close the gap in the defences at Sedan, beyond
Carignan. The vital bridge across the Meuse at this point
clearly had to be destroyed and over one hundred aircraft,
British and French, were lost when they were hurled at this
and associated targets. The result of this operation was the
most serious loss that the Royal Air Force has ever suffered

in a single day since the total casualties amounted to no less than 60 per cent of the British attackers, but what was to take place in the following few days was to be one of the early steps towards victory in what was later to be termed the Battle of Britain.

So dangerous was the situation now that the French Prime Minister, Paul Reynaud, himself only newly appointed on 21st March and a 62-year-old advocate of tank warfare who thought with the trained mind of a lawyer, was left with little alternative but to approach his almost equally new opposite number in Britain, Winston Churchill, and beg that further fighters be made available to stem the Nazi trickle which had suddenly become a deluge.

In reply to this Churchill, whatever his personal feelings as to the wisdom of such a move, had no choice but to support his ally and 15th May saw the despatch of a further six squadrons of Hawker Hurricanes to augment those already sent. This resulted in a total which was equivalent to ten squadrons having crossed the Channel in the previous few days, all equipped with Hawker Hurricanes as it was assumed that difficulties would be encountered on the atrocious surface of French airfields with the narrow track undercarriage of the Spitfire. Even so, despite the gravity of the situation, there was another impasse, due to the fact that some of the British Hurricanes, in order to meet the demands, had been drawn from amongst the earlier models. This meant that a percentage of those in use were fitted with, for instance, fixed-pitch, two-blade, wooden Watts airscrews and fabric-covered wings, both features discarded in the later variants.

While these reinforcements were yet to be deployed to repulse the Nazi advance, the enemy continued to press ahead with the support of the Luftwaffe which, in the manner established by experience in the earlier conflict only twenty-two years before, was closely wedded to the Army in the field. It was only the day following, 16th May, that Hugh Dowding, Fighter Command's 58-year-old Air

Officer Commanding-in-Chief, sat down on a bright May morning to dictate what was to be one of the most important documents in the history of England.

Addressed to the Under Secretary of State, the letter was only part, although perhaps the catalystic part, of a war that Dowding was waging with the Cabinet to retain a workable force of squadrons for the defence of Britain. There was a danger, he believed, that what the French really wanted was the committal of the entire British fighter arm to the defence of their country, this to come under not British but French command. That this danger was very real he felt there was ample evidence, for not only was Winston Churchill under massive personal pressure to grant the French request but also in the atmosphere of desperation that had now become part of life across the Channel, demands were received in Great Britain from a wide variety of official French sources, even commanders in the field who felt that the extreme gravity of the situation permitted a personal approach. In fact the position was such that—let there be no shadow of doubt on this point—had the strength of Fighter Command been further eroded, in the coming battle it would have unquestionably been vanquished in the same manner as the air forces of Poland and western Europe: swiftly, utterly and completely.

The letter followed a Cabinet meeting on 15th May when the point of the Hurricane wastage had been forcibly put by Dowding, but he was now in a stronger position due to the efforts of Cyril Newall, who had been appointed Chief of Air Staff in September 1937 and who had now achieved a compromise which permitted the six last committed squadrons to operate from bases in southern England, only landing to refuel and re-arm on the Continent.

Although Dowding's letter was despatched formally to the Air Ministry it was aimed at Churchill himself and in ten formal paragraphs it pointed out in courteous but fearless terms that the drain on Fighter Command that had taken place up to that time had already reduced its strength below the minimum necessary for the defence of Great Britain, a figure estimated by the Air Council itself to have been already eroded by sixteen squadrons.

Despite the "hope and belief" that Hugh Dowding expressed in his letter of the final victory of the Allies in France, this was no more than the courtesy of an earlier age and the inevitable gesture of a senior officer to morale. He was in fact under no illusion that France had been beaten and his mood at the time was close to despair.

Churchill had assumed the office of Prime Minister as recently as 10th May. He swiftly established the practice of meeting personally his counterparts in order to examine the situation which was deteriorating by the hour and Dowding's letter was received on the day following a visit by the Prime Minister to Paris. Here he had found his worst fears realized, for although Paul Reynaud felt strongly that no thought should be given to the question of an armistice with Hitler, he seemed to lack the strength of character to sway those among his colleagues who argued the case for such a course of action with increasing emphasis.

Arriving as it did within hours of Winston Churchill's home-coming, the effect of the letter from Fighter Command's chief was immediate, and after a Cabinet meeting when the whole subject was discussed a minute from Churchill recorded the fateful decision that whatever the needs of France, "No more squadrons of fighters will leave this country."

Although the tenacity of Dowding had achieved the first victory in the battle which was yet to come in company with a threat more gargantuan than any with which his Command's No. 11 Group had yet dealt, the process of scene-setting against which the grim drama was to be played out continued across the English Channel, and the British public was left in no doubt as to the seriousness of the situation. On 17th May many newspapers splashed across their front pages the announcement of an "Intense Battle around Sedan" and the inevitable cry of a beleagured people that they have suffered betrayal seemed echoed by the *News Chronicle*'s announcement that a new strong man was sought to head the French Republic's army by the headline "Weygand Replaces Gamelin". The British media were certainly more explicit than their French counterparts. The issue of *Le Temps* for the fateful Thursday said, "Our fighters dominate, perhaps even more, the enemy air force", an example of an attempt to keep up public morale that had reached the point where readers were misled.

On the same day that the new French general had assumed command the advancing 6th, 7th and 8th Panzer Divisions were only a few miles east of Laon, and showed every sign of sweeping beyond Abbeville within a few days, a point that they and other divisions had passed on the road to Boulogne by 22nd May. This manoeuvre trapped not only the 1st, 7th and 9th Armies of the British Expeditionary Force, but three of those of France and what remained of the Belgian Army. The latter had received a severe mauling, but the gallantry of that country's stand at the beginning of the earlier war was never allowed to become a dim memory by the news media, which spilled much emotional ink to this end.

Meanwhile with their rapidly extending corridor along the Aisne and Somme the Nazis knew that a counter-attack was inevitable, so they were surprised when attempts to sever their line of communication came relatively late. Two attacks were launched by the French 4th Armoured Division that was commanded by a tall, gaunt colonel with a striking presence. His name was Charles de Gaulle but as yet there was no indication that the name was to pass into history.

Certainly other counter-attacks had been planned and an early one had been ordered by General Gamelin though cancelled by the elderly general that succeeded him.

Operation Dynamo, intended to lift the British Armies from Dunkirk and nearby ports, had been started five days earlier when the announcement was made on 28th May that

Belgium was about to capitulate, and there were many who could only believe that such a report was a rumour, for such a course of action seemed unthinkable. In fact the cease-fire had taken place at 0400 hours on the previous day and many a Belgian soldier felt that his King had deserted him as he watched with tear-filled eyes his battle colours being smuggled to a place of safety or destroyed along with the piles of documents that might be of use to the victorious enemy, now able to threaten the British Armies on two sides of a triangle while the sea formed the third.

Anticipating that this was the sole avenue of escape, only three days before the first troops were lifted from the beaches, Churchill had ordered that a large number of small vessels be assembled to ferry the men from the shelving sands to the larger ships, and as the pressure continued increasing numbers of British servicemen fell back in the direction of Dunkirk.

The turn of events in Belgium put the British press in something of a quandary. The death of the King of the Belgians who had ruled in 1914, in a mountaineering accident twenty years later, had created a great deal of sympathy for King Albert's family and this had been heightened in the next year when his son's Queen, the Swedish Princess Astrid, a girl of striking beauty, had been killed in a car accident. Now it was necessary for the media to perform a complete public about-turn, and writers and commentators turned on the luckless King Leopold savagely, openly describing him in a less mealy-mouthed age than our own as "treacherous".

Be that as it may, the surrender did more than yield Belgium to the enemy, it also sealed the fate of the 1st French Army immediately, for both its flanks were now left unprotected. However, so heroic was the resistance of the doomed Frenchmen that when the inevitable happened and surrender could no longer be avoided the opposing General Waeger ordered that his enemies be saluted with a guard of honour.

The advance of the Wehrmacht west and south was yet to come so some reinforcements were being sent from Great Britain at the same time as the bulk of the BEF was being taken from Dunkirk. However, Operation Dynamo was not confined to taking troops from this port alone, another thus used being Brest with its magnificent harbour.

An airman who departed from thence was Bill Jones, who had gone to France with the Mechanical Transport Section of No. 615 Squadron as recently as November 1939, there being some from this same unit that had been in France since the outbreak of war. The cathedral at Rheims had only just been restored and reconsecrated, he recalls, after four years of bombardment in the earlier war, but now the roads of that city, like those of Le Mans, were crammed with civilians so that motorized vehicles took from dawn to dusk to complete a journey of perhaps eighty miles.

Many of the civilians were begging for food, often for children whose unceasing cries could be heard even over the sound of the lorry engines. Down the middle of the road perhaps stumbled old people already supporting them-selves on sticks and now footsore as, like blind automatons, they goaded their stiffened limbs to continued effort. Some were completely incapable of walking and Jones recalls the sight of an old woman who pushed her husband in a wheel-barrow, its course winding and unsteady as weariness overcame the man's wife.

Many of these refugees were abandoning nearly all their possessions and clutched only those few household goods that they had seized in their panic and thrust into a pillow-case that they now hung on to as the last vestiges of the life they had known. For many of these it was their second experience of this sort of thing, having fled before the advancing enemy twenty-five summers before, and for the servicemen that tried to push their way through it was all like the re-enactment of some nightmare film. Men like Corporal Skidmore, armourer and Gallipoli veteran, who at forty-two was an old man to the teenagers in his charge, found little was changed except the aircraft that were now Hawker Hurricanes instead of the Ninaks and Bristol Fighters of their previous time in France. Hair's-breadth escapes were as commonplace as before: for example, Aircraftman Belcher marched out of Abbeville on Monday 20th May as the Nazi troops entered via the east gate at the other end of the town, thus typifying the attitude which was to stand the British serviceman in good stead in the months to come for discipline was nearly always maintained and the withdrawal was in no way an example of mass panic.

It was night when the British lorries first entered Brest but the summer dawn was sufficiently close for a dreadful spectacle for any fighting man to be made out. Every turning off the main road both within the town and along the approaches was lined with abandoned British equipment, not only lorries and transport vehicles of all sorts but also 25-pounder field guns.

The journey to Brest had originally been intended to be one to St Nazaire but the vehicle that Bill Jones drove had been stopped by the Military Police and directions had been given for the new destination since St Nazaire was even then in enemy hands, so swift had been the Nazi advance.

Now, as the first light of the May morning was just lighting the horizon, the drivers, most of whom had not moved from the cabs of their trucks for two days, were ordered to freshen up and they washed and shaved in the cold water of a pond, although these primitive ablutions did nothing to relieve their smarting eyes where weariness made them feel as if quantities of grit were lodged.

The sight that most took the attention of the new arrivals was the activities of the Pioneer Corps, who worked for complete days without stopping, shifting material. For the most part they were men of less than average height but wiry and by now they appeared to have been reduced almost to robots as they drove themselves on despite the overwhelming desire for rest, their sole sustenance, it seemed, being tea and rum, the latter salvaged from casks "accidentally" damaged.

At Brest came the unhappy task of making useless to the enemy the motor vehicles that had served their crews so well and this was usually done by smashing the engines with hammers or draining the sumps of oil and then running the motors until they seized up. Meanwhile soldiers continued to pour into the town to mingle with the RAF men already there. Many of the former had been roaming the countryside without their weapons either singly or in small groups, living as best they could but always making for the coast, the aimless remnants of a demoralized army. Yet there were exceptions, for here and there orderly lines of men in disciplined ranks and with their equipment intact swung through the confusion of the refugee-blocked roads; frequently these men proved to be from the Brigade of Guards but whatever their unit they made a striking contrast with the French soldiers, who would bolt like panic-stricken wild beasts at the appearance of an aircraft at low altitude whether it was friend or foe.

It was now that the "little ships", which have passed into history and had imaginatively been mustered at Churchill's personal suggestion, came into their own. Many of them were pressed into use running a shuttle-service to the larger vessels anchored some distance off the shore due to the long shelving beach, and a large number were lost in this work since the captive Army was pounded by the Nazi Luftwaffe. Meanwhile the RAF, flying from bases in southern England, did their best, despite the bitterness of many soldiers at the seeming absence of fighter protection, to keep the enemy at bay.

In contrast to the method of escape experienced by many, Bill Jones made his way home in the hold of a coal boat normally employed to take fuel to Battersea Power Station. The remnants of its last load were still under the deck and he and other RAF men shared the discomfort there with some kilted Scots Canadian soldiers, one of whom carried a kitten he had somewhere rescued in the safety of his blouse, for only the machine gunners were allowed on deck.

Home for this particular load of exhausted men was Plymouth after an uneventful crossing, unlike many, and after a wait outside the harbour while hospital ships discharged. These men, who had not eaten for seven hours, were greeted by the welcome sight of the Salvation Army distributing tea, "wads" and a postcard on which to write home—no stamp was required: in the atmosphere of the day to write "BEF" in its place was sufficient.

While these more fortunate men were resting shattered nerves and wearied bodies in a hangar at Filton where row after row of beds had been laid out, there were still thousands less lucky who, perhaps after giving themselves the illusion of protection by scooping a foxhole in the soft sand, could do no more than wait. Occasionally they were to see a welcome sight as when one of the enemy was destroyed, and one rifleman can still recall the cheer that rolled like a wave of sound across the crowded beach when a Stuka met its end against the background of the massive pall of black smoke that rose all day and all night from the oil storage tanks set alight in the town. The Junkers 87 had first appeared at about 15,000 feet and had begun its near vertical dive when a Spitfire appeared and closed at a shallower angle, for to follow one of these dive-bombers down was useless: the pursuer merely went screaming down only to flash past his intended victim. On this occasion the enemy pilot had released his bomb beyond some dunes and was climbing away in the comparative quiet when the "Jericho trumpets'"* ceased, when it was raked by fire from the Spitfire's Brownings, cutting away the wings of the Nazi machine.

Yet while this sort of thing was going on there were other, smaller, unsung forms of heroism taking place, made all the more difficult by the fact that by now telephone

* Wind-driven "screamers" on the undercarriage legs operated during a bombing dive to increase the din and further demoralize those in the target area.

communication was almost non-existent. This included the salvaging of lightly damaged British fighters left by the Advanced Air Striking Force, and although the majority were either damaged beyond repair or put to the torch some, with Heath Robinson-type repairs effected with perhaps the aid of wire and telephone cable, were patched up sufficiently to limp across the Channel. But even once airborne the troubles of the pilots were by no means over for the troops below were apt to empty their rifles at anything that flew, perhaps in the belief that the British half-black and half-white undersurfaces applied as an easy recognition feature indicated an unfamiliar and therefore enemy colour scheme.

Soon all was over and although it was a miracle of deliverance it was also unquestionably a defeat, a fact that Winston Churchill was at pains to point out, for although a grand total of 366,162 men, Allied and French, were taken from the beaches, moles and harbours, about 40,000 could not be saved and had to be left to face life in prison camps. To this should be added the 28,000 or so killed or wounded, the dead being left to mingle their bones with those of their fathers which could be found still under a few inches of rich French soil. The flares that illuminated the beaches at night to aid Nazi bombers were to go out and men no longer howled at their fellows not to stand up, their shattered nerves making them believe illogically that an upright figure among a thousand recumbent ones was an aid to bomb-aimers.

All this the newspapers duly reported to their British readers until On Wednesday 5th June, one announced: "Dunkirk: The End", for the day before Nazi troops had marched into the town at the same time as the Luftwaffe had bombed Paris, causing a reported 290 casualties. Four days earlier there were only 283 serviceable aircraft available at airfields in southern England, the bulk of them together with the 362 pilots at No. 11 Group's bases. Small wonder that one newspaper not given to sensationalism summed up the position with the chilling phrase "Backs to the Wall".

For France the future held nothing but humiliation; for the men who had left her, each in his private cocoon of fear, had abandoned the country to a crumbling administration within and a ruthless enemy flushed with victory that saw Paris as the final goal. The same day as the dreadful phrase had appeared on many a British breakfast-table, the Wehrmacht seemed to redouble its efforts so that the advance north-west along the Aisne was now repeated in the opposite direction by part of the XVI Panzer Corps and the XIV Motorized Corps which were finally to make a lunge in the direction of Rheims five days later when Buisson's counter-attack, the only determined attempt to stem the advance in this sector, was beaten off. On 13th June the Motorized Corps had reached Romilly, while further to the east the enemy had passed St Dizier.

Meanwhile the advance to the west continued so that Rouen was reached on 9th June, the two arms of the thrust thus effectively placing Paris in a ring of steel despite the huge attempt to stop the advance that the French mounted at Amiens. The enemy to the north still had the task of driving north-west and thus spring a trap for the Allied troops cornered along that part of the northern French coast.

In the situation thus created it is no surprise that mid June found Paul Reynaud unable to rally his dispirited government so that he had little alternative but to hand to President Lebrun at the Prefecture of the Gironde his resignation, which also named as his successor the aged Marshal Pétain. Here, it was thought, was a man who could pluck victory from the jaws of defeat, for he had earned for himself the name of the saviour of the French Army that had been so close to complete collapse twenty-three years before. Now, however, his plans were seen by many as the work of a traitor since they could be summed up in the words of one commentator of the time who described the old marshal as saving France for no one but Nazi Germany. This proved to be exactly his policy and one of his first acts was to approach Hitler with a request for armistice terms.

Examination of these proved them to be of the most humiliating type and the eight points set out in the document demanded nothing less than the demobilization of both the French and foreign armies in the country, coupled with an actual occupation or subjugation of the nation.

All seemed lost, and abroad indeed was, but it was to the surprise of many that a new French voice was suddenly to be heard, this time from England, that of none other than the same Charles de Gaulle who had been involved so recently in the fighting. Now he was a general and had been Reynaud's Under-Secretary for War. In a broadcast on 18th June he took it upon himself to lead those of his countrymen who were determined to carry on the fight in exile, his final words summing up the situation exactly when he said: "Notre patrie est en péril de mort. Luttons tous pour la sauver!" (Our country is in danger of death. Let us all fight to save it!)

What de Gaulle said of his own land was now substantially true of the whole of western Europe, to which was added that same June the Channel Islands which fell to Hitler without a shot being fired. It was perfectly obvious that the next step would be the invasion of the British Isles, the first time that the country had been threatened by a foe since the days of Napoleon. The mood of the country changed almost overnight: petty differences were set aside under the common danger and an atmosphere of defiance took hold so that even an innocent journalist who purchased a local map to find the best way to get his stories back to London when the invader struck, found himself interviewed by the Dover Police within a very short time.

As not for two hundred years, Britain was now at bay, and preparations rapidly took place to prepare for the worst that seemed inevitable. Town and district names disappeared along with anything else that would help the enemy paratroops, and as a preliminary to the actual fighting—some of which would have to be carried out by the new LDVs, Local Defence Volunteers, later the Home Guard—pillboxes appeared in town and country, some of them camouflaged to look like shops and outbuildings, while alongside these there grew like overnight mushrooms strange cylindrical objects—smoke-screen generators.

"If the INVADER comes," announced a leaflet put through every letterbox in the kingdom, "what to do—and how to do it." But the possibility of invasion (and in the hearts and minds of the majority it was more a probability) hinged on a single factor—no enemy troops could be put ashore, no troop carriers could drop parachutists and no Nazi tanks could rumble through the roads and lanes of Sussex, Kent and Surrey, from where the Channel was at its narrowest, until it was safe for them to do so with any chance of success; and that safety could only be given by the protection of the Nazi Luftwaffe, so that it was first necessary for the Royal Air Force to be driven from the skies of England in the way that the air arms of the other countries had so recently been vanquished. The next move was therefore the destruction of the RAF's fighter force and this largely meant southern England's No. 11 Group.

CHAPTER TWO

The Commanders

It was not until 1936 that the Fighter Command of the Royal Air Force came into existence. It was a time when a large number of politicians still believed in the Ten-year Rule, a comfortable supposition that there would be no major war in Europe for that period of time, which was calculated, subject to the prevailing military situation, from whatever point in time one happened to be. This was a policy which was encouraged by the Treasury since it enabled that body to do nothing "at the present".

With the formation of new Commands it was necessary that the one responsible for the defence of the kingdom should have some workable sub-divisions and these took the form of Groups, of which the most important, since it defended the capital itself, was unquestionably No. 11, covering the whole of south-east England.

Selected as AOC-in-C of the new Fighter Command was

a little-known officer, 54-year-old Hugh Caswell Tremenheere Dowding, who had previously been an Air Marshal on the Air Council with responsibility for Supply and Research. Brought up in a scholastic atmosphere—his father had been a schoolmaster and many of his family were clergymen—Dowding had been educated at Winchester before going on to New College, Oxford.

In September 1899 Dowding had sat the entrance examination for the Royal Military Woolwich where, instead of the expected two-year course, he took one shortened to a single year because of the demands then being made by the Boer War. Here, although certainly of the right material for a commission in the Royal Engineers, he in fact received the rank of Second Lieutenant in the Garrison Artillery, later attributing his failure to enter the Royal Engineers to laziness. However that might have been the young eighteen-and-a-half-year-old officer was beginning a career which was to culminate in his saving from the aggressor the country of his birth and which was to place him on the same footing as such men as Wellington and Nelson. Yet for all this, it is a regrettable fact that today only a minority can immediately recall his name, so he is in this respect in much the same position as his sixteenth-century equivalent, Lord Howard of Effingham, the admiral who commanded the fleet opposing the might of the Spanish Armada.

Dowding's career now took him to Gibraltar, then to Ceylon. Here he learned to play polo, thus proving unquestionably his qualities of physical courage, for, unless one has tried it, it is impossible to imagine just what a swift mind, what sure co-ordination and raw attack the game calls for. It was in the years following this period, after transfer to the Mountain Artillery had taken him to India, that another quality began to show itself. In common with many of West Country stock, for example, Francis Drake three hundred and more years before, Hugh Dowding showed a certain independence of view and although discipline demanded the obligatory deference to rank, he took no pains to conceal the belief that certain of his superiors were not of his own intellectual standing.

That this must have been a difficult realization to live with is made all the more clear by the fact that Hugh Dowding was an essentially shy man, so that he was not capable of joining in the more light-hearted undertakings of his brother officers, with the result that he was quickly given the nickname which was to persist for the remainder of his life: "Stuffy". This is not to say that he disapproved of high spirits, quite the opposite in fact, it was just that he lacked the ability to take the plunge and join in. Thus he tended to stand aside and seemingly endorse the unfortunate label. Air Marshal Sir Gerald Gibbs, second-in-command of No. 11 Group in 1940, summed up this side of Dowding's character for the author with the words, ". . . though his nickname was 'Stuffy' I personally never found him so."

After six years in India, Hugh finally entered the Military Staff College at Camberley, Surrey, following the last of a number of applications which were turned down, and it was the following year, 1913, that he learned to fly. The reason for this was typical since he had become interested in the new art but was astonished at the lack of interest, even hostility, - that the Army in general displayed towards aviation. In common with others at this time instruction was at his own expense, although a refund was given to successful candidates after they had qualified. Another facet of his character was shown at this time by the arrangements which he made with the flying school that they would be paid *after* he had passed through the Central Flying School at Upavon.

Not only was Hugh Dowding an intensely practical man but the very fact that he wished to become a pilot, despite the atmosphere of hide-bound conservatism in which he found himself, shows the possession of great forward vision, a quality that was to stand the country in good stead, not only with regard to the question of fighters for France that has already been discussed but also in another field, as will be related later.

Following the outbreak of war in 1914, Major Dowding, who had been on the Royal Flying Corps Reserve, found himself in France in command of No. 16 Squadron equipped at the time with BE2c aircraft after its formation at St Omer in February 1915. With this artillery observation unit, Dowding was not popular, a fact that may in part have been due to his being an undistinguished pilot and seldom flew, but in the main because of his shyness, so that his own reserve tended to stifle enthusiasm. Yet among the eighteen-year-olds he commanded—he now being a little less than double that age—there were those who realized that he was a good man and an efficient officer, calm, strict and with a sense of duty, although the picture that Duncan Grinnell-Milne paints of his commander is of a seemingly austere figure with a thin sandy-coloured head whom he likens to a melancholy bird. The familiar nickname was unused in No. 16 Squadron but it was replaced by another, equally uncomplimentary: "The Starched Shirt".

Yet despite the superficial estimation of Hugh Dowding's character the real man was very different, and Grinnell-Milne came near to getting some of it right. For one thing, he had a ready wit of a dry and penetrating nature, which could suddenly flash out to enliven a sombre situation. During the coming battle when he was to distinguish himself in 1940 it was he who established the atmosphere of confidence, nonchalance even, that spread through the Headquarters staff, although his own feelings at the time, as he was later to state, on occasion approached despair.

At the end of the First World War, Dowding found himself Chief Staff Officer, first in the Inland Area and then in Iraq, appointments to be followed by several posts abroad before he assumed command of the Fighting Area of the old Air Defence of Great Britain. Despite these duties, his personal bent had always been towards the technical, indeed it was a misunderstanding between himself and

Major-General Trenchard, General Officer commanding the RFC in France, that had brought about his removal to Great Britain from France when he had personally tested a Maurice Farman fitted with a doubtful type of airscrew. Posted to command the Administrative Wing at Farnborough he was admirably suited to the work involved, for his experience in France included trials in the field of airborne wireless and investigations into the reason for a number of crashes of Blériot monoplanes when the pilots (including himself) had succumbed to the effects of the exhaust fumes.

The incisive and technical mind with which he was gifted, reflected in his mode of speech which was clear and precisely articulated, placed him in a position whereby he achieved his first victory for 1940, not during that hot summer nor even when he was assuming the role of Churchill's inflexible mentor, but in the days of peace before a shot had been fired.

Matters had begun when investigations were ordered in 1934 into the feasibility of producing an ultimate weapon capable of emitting "death-rays", a device which was offered in many forms to the defences at regular intervals. None of these worked but their likelihood was to be finally looked into and the most practical form of these seemed to be found in the sphere of electro-magnetism. Copies of the memorandum urging thorough scientific examination of the suggestion were sent to the Chief of Air Staff and to Sir Hugh Dowding, then the Air Marshal in charge of Research and Development.

Also working about this time was a young scientist who had held several government posts mainly devoted to the question of tracking thunderstorms. His name was Robert Watson-Watt and his system was to listen to the register on a radio frequency of the electric charges from the associated lightning. This experience was to prove of great importance for although the idea of a "death-ray" proved impracticable, it did seem to point the way to a system of radio detection.

The trials that subsequently followed took the form of, in Dowding's own words, "shooting electric impulses into the air and catching them again when they bounced back off a kind of invisible ceiling in the upper air". (This ceiling was in fact the Heaviside Layer.) Although this description undoubtedly over-simplifies the work, the tests were sufficiently promising for a specially modified radio receiver with a cathode-ray tube for presenting the reflections visually to be assembled in a van in 1935 and driven off to Daventry, where a Heyford bomber had been sent from Farnborough, its pilot ordered to patrol a certain line at a predetermined altitude. Shut in the dark vehicle the blue-green signal was the focus of attention for all those crammed inside and sure enough, as the bomber crossed the radiated beam, its presence was registered on the cathode-ray tube, and it was a matter of minutes later that the sound of the motors announced to human ears the presence of the machine overhead. So great was the following excitement that it is said Watson-Watt forgot to pick up his young nephew deposited some way off in view of the secret nature of the tests, but it is certain that the results were reported as soon as possible to Dowding.

Here, quite clearly, was a system that superseded all the attempts to gain advance warning of aircraft approach from beyond the range of human sight and it was also manifestly superior to the sound-locators that had been in use in one form or another. There had even been a suggestion during the First World War by Lieutenant-Colonel Rawlinson, in charge of London's defences, that these instruments be manned by blind persons on account of their superior hearing.

Other tests had taken the form of the creation of enormous "sound mirrors", huge concave saucers to focus the sound of aircraft motors approaching from off the coast. These had at first been gouged out of the native chalk but later man-made versions had been laid down in concrete. Some would have been only 15 feet in diameter and ranged

out in line but others were to be double that size or even—
and this was more an acoustic wall—to extend for a distance
of 200 feet and be 25 feet tall, one such being assembled on
the beach at Dungeness and used in the 1934 Summer Air
Exercises when it proved more or less useless.

With this experience fresh in his mind, Dowding needed
little convincing of the importance of the trials, a "breakthrough" in modern parlance, and as Air Member for
Research and Development he had no hesitation in sanc-
tioning the expenditure of £10,000 by the Treasury for the
continuation of the work, this in the second half of the 1930s
being a not inconsiderable sum.

The invention was not known then as now by the name
radar, for that is an American term introduced later. From
about this time the system was known as RDF (Radio
Direction Finding) or simply Radiolocation, this being a
vaguely accurate description with a good security ring
about it, and it was under one or other of these contemporary descriptions that Dowding then continued to press
for the unrelenting perfection of the system. His experience
was such that he saw immediately that aircraft guided in
this way would be saved from the exhausting and wasteful
necessity of maintaining standing patrols, a system
whereby aircraft are kept on a regular celestial beat and
relieved from time to time in an effort to reduce the chances
of an enemy slipping past in the vastness of the bowl of the
sky, perhaps in poor weather or reduced visibility.

Having said so much about the hitherto disgracefully
"unsung" Dowding, it is necessary to take a closer look at
some of his personal qualities. In part these have already
been mentioned but there remain two questions to be
answered. Firstly, why, despite the undoubted standing of
his achievement, was there, throughout the period that we
now know was the summit of his career, a measure of
unco-operation from the Air Ministry? It has been
suggested that at the actual time of the Battle of Britain the
officers of the Air Staff did not appreciate the significance of

what was happening, so that it was not until the whole picture could be viewed that they began to realize that, in the words of the Duke of Wellington after another victory that ensured Great Britain's survival, it had been "a damned close thing". This was the feeling amongst many at No. 11 Group at the actual time, an important point to note, as it is easy to be wise with the advantage of hindsight.

Why the Air Ministry took the attitude it did may be readily explained by reference to the officers who made up the Air Staff at the time. They were mostly airmen who had received their experience in the bomber field rather than that of the fighter. It had also been argued that this arrangement was as it should be for although the summer of 1940 ended with the Royal Air Force having wrested a victory from the Luftwaffe, it was victory in a battle in the *defence* of this country, and no war has ever yet been won by this means alone; it is only a method of buying time until an offensive, which alone can win a war, may be begun and it is just this latter that the minds of staff officers were and must always be preoccupied with. It is part of history now that both Dowding and Sir Keith Park were treated with something less than their due after the vanquishing of the enemy in the air and the above reasons for the initial attitude may also have something to do with the sad state of affairs which removed both from their commands before the end of the year when they had achieved so much, some said the impossible.

The second question of interest is, what was the personal relationship that existed between the AOC-in-C of Fighter Command and Winston Churchill? In looking into this it is an important if readily overlooked fact that at the time Winston Churchill was very new to his post. He had come to power when Great Britain was in the most perilous position for several hundred years; all her allies had vanished in swift and terrible succession and the country, with a beaten and depleted army, was facing at a distance of only a little over twenty miles of sea a foe, well organized, equipped as well as any in the world and with men whose spirits and self-esteem could not have been higher.

The elevation of Winston Churchill to the position of the country's leader, where he could encourage and put into words the defiance and determination that men most needed at the time, was not greeted with unalloyed enthusiasm in all the corridors of power. For many years he had been the *enfant terrible* of the political world and the period in the wilderness of party politics had tended to add to this feeling, so there were doubtless some who, at least at that time, were in fear of Churchill. Hugh Dowding was not one of these but he had been obliged to back his personal judgement of the new Prime Minister to the hilt when he had forced the issue of the extra fighters for France and in this he had adopted the policy of the school of officers from which he came, determined, unflinching, calm and with a logical and militarily calculating mind.

Although Winston Churchill was no lover of yes-men, the number of the Dowding calibre up against whom he had come in life were few and a random look at these seems to throw up only Robert Baden-Powell as a likely candidate for similarity, and neither he nor Churchill had found the other's qualities endearing. Nevertheless Churchill found Dowding to be a man who, while lacking that slight touch of the attractive eccentric that made himself the expressive showman, still displayed many of his own characteristics of integrity, unswerving devotion to duty and tenacity. Yet despite this, or perhaps because of it, the two great men never became friends. This was partly due to the fact that Churchill had a built-in distrust of senior officers born of experience with some of rather limited intelligence, while Dowding for his part had no particular love of politicians, a healthy and not uncommon attitude in servicemen. But there was one overriding fact and this was that Dowding had openly opposed the new Prime Minister and had forced him to make a policy U-turn in the full glare of the political light and at a critical time, so that there could never be more to their future relationship than a certain correct courtesy.

To say this is not to denigrate either man. Each recognized the other's qualities and it is surely moving into the realms of sentiment to wish to discover that behind the scenes they enjoyed a close friendship.

Today all this is a long time ago and had the summer of 1940 and No. 11 Group's contribution to it not been unique in Britain's history all would long ago have been relegated to the dust which attracts only scholars. Some idea of the time-scale involved may be arrived at when it is stated that the historic year was nearer in time to the first flight by the Wright brothers than the space which divides us from the Battle of Britain, but there is today in each of our homes strange echoes of Dowding's first step along the road to victory. These are our television sets, for it was no public gesture that prompted the announcement in 1935 by the Postmaster-General that a London television service would be established—there were darker undertones. The head-start that Britain achieved over the rest of the world when the first television service was begun on 2nd November 1936 with the transmissions from Alexandra Palace was achieved with startling suddenness because in this way it was possible to ensure that the manufacture of cathode ray tubes, suitable for RDF sets, would quickly be brought to production standard.

The first dull rumblings of the Munich Crisis which were to send the ageing Neville Chamberlain to Berchtesgaden in September to buy time for Britain were in the air when during the summer of 1938 the commanding officer of the fighter station at RAF Tangmere received a new posting to become Dowding's Senior Air Staff Officer. This was New Zealander Keith Rodney Park, son of Professor James Park, the younger man having come to England to serve as a gunner during the First World War.

Like so many others he had transferred in 1917 to the Royal Flying Corps but it was not until the war had been over for two years that he received the command of his first squadron, and this was followed by a course at the RAF Staff College before he was sent to Buenos Aires as air attaché.

With the rank of air commodore in 1938, Park brought with him to Fighter Command's headquarters a vast knowledge of fighters, for most of his service career had been spent in this field, and Park and Dowding worked exceptionally well together despite the discrepancy in their ages, Park being forty-five while his chief was exactly eleven years his senior. The complete harmony that existed between the two men undoubtedly speeded the rapid build-up of the operational side of the new command and perhaps their common outlook as former gunners had something to do with this, although more likely reasons were their shared level of intelligence and a realization that time to consolidate Britain's defences was fast running out.

The partnership lasted until the spring of 1940 when Keith Park was promoted to command that same No. 11 Group that he had helped to create and in his new capacity he swiftly became popular with his subordinates, partly due to his being far more articulate than his old chief, but in a large measure due to his enormous capacity for hard work coupled with an easy manner and a slow smile that took the sting out of many a highly charged situation. However, none of this is to say that Keith Park was in any way soft or easy-going and in the months to come many a junior officer at fighter stations in southern England had cause to remember that the lean figure who had arrived in an unannounced Hurricane fighter turned out to be wearing the insignia of the No. 11 Group commander under his white flying overalls.

This habit of seeing at first hand how matters lay had begun over the beaches of Dunkirk. As a result of what he observed there he sought permission to operate a maximum of four squadrons at any one time to cover the evacuation after 29th May, although this placed a heavy burden on the total squadron muster of which this figure represented a quarter, so that only limited operations were possible since 250 Hurricane fighters had already been lost over the beaches between 8th May and mid-month. Nevertheless Britain's strength in the air was relatively strong compared with the Army's position.

His loyalty to Dowding was beyond question, for the two had come to understand each other's problems intimately during the last days of peace when they had laboured together to ensure that at least the majority of fighters had VHF radios to replace the old HF models (a battle in which the two were only partly successful), heated guns and an adequacy of belt links, there being a gross shortage of these at the time of Munich.

But if there was no question about the loyalty of the devout Keith Park who, despite the anguish of the daily decisions in the battle to come, always found time for private prayer from which he seemed to draw inspiration, his opposite number commanding No. 12 Group, which lay to the north of the area that was to bear the brunt of the Luftwaffe's assault possessed quite different characteristics.

For those who wish to know the story of a man's life and career there is no worse source than his obituary. At best this has been written to give the minimum pain to his surviving family and at worst there seems to be a subconscious determination to deceive a celestial gatekeeper into admitting an undeserving candidate. Coupled to this, should a man merit an obituary in wartime the position is further confused, for the notes on his life are composed with the additional overtone of their propaganda value and the desire to give little help to an enemy.

Such is the case which makes it all the more difficult to judge the officer who commanded No. 11 Group's neighbour, Trafford Leigh-Mallory, who had been put in charge of No. 12 Group in 1937. Ambitious and self-opinionated, he had a great enthusiasm for the proper respect due to his

APPROX RDF LIMITS:
TO   5OO Ft.   ----
TO 15,OOO Ft.   —·—

●—GROUP HQ
12— GROUP
      IDENTITY

No. 11 Group and its neighbouring areas

own rank yet was not above unbecoming criticism of his colleagues and superiors, so much so in fact that when matters such as this became public knowledge, Dowding, who had been in ignorance of the situation for a long time, giving all his Group commanders his equal confidence, is on record as having remarked that he ought to have dismissed Leigh-Mallory.

The choice of this officer to command a Fighter Group surprised many for his Air Force experience had, back to his being seconded to the Royal Flying Corps in 1916, been mainly concerned with Army Co-operation work.

The story of the personal vendetta that he waged against the victorious Keith Park has frequently been told elsewhere and it finally bore fruit when he was given the command of Park's Group, which it seems Leigh-Mallory had always regarded as his right. Keith Park was familiar with the situation from the very earliest days of his own command but, rightly or wrongly, he made no report of the matter to his superior, which he would have been perfectly within his rights to do. Part of the reason was because it would have added yet another responsibility to his already over-burdened AOC-in-C, who both at the time and throughout the Battle of Britain was constantly under the threat of being retired for reasons of age, the actual and final date being continuously put forward by short periods of time.

What is perhaps less commonly known is the fact that when Sir Trafford Leigh-Mallory had finally secured the command of No. 11 Group in 1942—in part with the backing of Sir Archibald Sinclair, who, although appointed as Secretary of State for Air in May 1940 had only slight knowledge of the services gained during a course at the Royal Military College, Sandhurst, and while a Major in the 2nd Life Guards, coupled with none whatsoever of aviation—the new AOC of 11 Group had his theories put to the test during an exercise mounted to analyse the victory in the air fighting of two summers before. The result was a disaster.

Before being promoted further into the very post of Air Officer Commanding in Chief of Fighter Command which had so ably been filled by the redoubtable Dowding, Sir Trafford had a major operation on his hands in the form of the escape up the English Channel of the Nazi warships* *Scharnhorst, Gneisenau* and *Prinz Eugen*. For this he had prepared with meticulous planning a sphere of operations for which he had an undoubted gift, but these preparations were based on the assumption of a sortie under cover of darkness although in fact the escape was made in daylight, as many had predicted. Yet fairness demands that Sir Trafford be credited with creating an offensive Fighter Command which proved almost impregnable in 1944 at the time of the Allied invasion of Nazi-held Europe.

Hugh Dowding strongly regarded himself as part of a team, albeit the leader, and any investigation in depth must prove that such is the case. It would therefore be grossly unfair to close this chapter without reference to two other men who made their own, and quite differing, contribution to the victory of No. 11 Group and its associates.

The first of these is Sir Gerald Gibbs, who before becoming Keith Park's Senior Air Staff Officer and therefore second-in-command of No. 11 Group, was at one time working in Air Staff Plans at a time when Britain's defences were still bedevilled by the "ten-year dictum", which prevented the implementation of measures that could have been introduced relatively cheaply.

It was May 1940 when Sir Gerald was ordered to take charge of Filton, the sector station near Bristol, and a part of No. 10 Group commanded by Sir Quintin Brand; only hours before departure for the new post he was told in a telephone call from the Chief of Personnel at the Air Ministry to wait a week or two and then go to No. 11 Group as its deputy commander. As events turned out much of his work was very similar to that performed by his chief,

---

* Dealt with in detail in *Operation Thunderbolt* (Robert Hale, 1981) by the same author.

entailing the gathering of information from fighter stations on the spot and the pooling of advice and assistance, the nature of such measures being told in a succeeding chapter. Just how wise was the choice of such an able officer and how great the responsibility will be realized when it is stated that during August Keith Park fell ill and was away on sick leave for about two weeks, during which time Gerald Gibbs was appointed as AOC and took full responsibility for conducting the air war during that time over southern England. This he did with few concerns beyond those to which he had become used but something of the strain of the momentous days may be judged from the fact that over the complete period between the final evacuation of British forces from Europe and the onset of the campaign of Nazi night bombing, his weight dropped by twenty-eight pounds.

But however many and bold the fighters' pilots may be and however excellent and reliable the work of the ground technicians without whom all else is useless, even under the most able of leaderships, nothing can be achieved if the aircraft are without fuel in huge quantities. There is a story that when Poland was about to be engulfed by the Nazi army, and the normal supplies of spirit were lost, in some areas children were sent out with cans to steal it from wherever they could.

To ensure that such a situation did not develop in this country—and in the days when all petrol products were imported it might very well have happened—the organization of part of the fuel supply system was placed in the hands of the British oil-executive 27-year-old James Alexander Hulme who had entered the industry in Trinidad. He it was who at the beginning of the Second World War took charge of the creation and operation of Britain's first aviation fuel refinery, making a massive contribution to what was in fact the first major defeat of the war for Nazi Germany in so doing.

CHAPTER THREE

No. 11 Group

On its creation in June 1936 the new Fighter Command of the Royal Air Force was organized geographically into Groups, these being directly under the command of headquarters situated at Bentley Priory, Stanmore, in Middlesex. The northern boundary of the Group that was to bear the brunt of the coming conflict ran from Great Yarmouth to Duxford in Cambridgeshire before proceeding due west to protect London's northern flank. The western boundary took a line southwards between Oxford and Reading before veering off to terminate at the coast east of Bournemouth.

Beyond these boundaries were the areas of neighbouring Groups. No. 12 lay to the north with, beyond, No. 13 Group, while the defence of the south-west of the country was in the care of No. 10 Group, which was due to become operational in July.

The original Group commander of No. 11 area was Air Vice-Marshal Sir Philip Jourbert de la Ferté, the former AOC HQ, Fighting Area, which was the predecessor of the Group that had undergone only a few changes since it had been established after the First World War, when the primary threat was seen to be directed from France. It is plain that the layout of the new Group was based loosely on that of the old system, for the actual sector of sky where it was assumed interceptions would be made was sandwiched between a pair of artillery zones, the Fighting Area being divided into sectors, these being ten in number.

In the same manner the new No. 11 Group was divided into six sectors, five of these radiating towards the coast from that north-west of London. The strength of the Group was supplied by twelve squadrons, Nos 1, 17, 19, 23, 25, 32, 43, 54, 56, 65, 66 and 111, these being based at Biggin Hill, Hornchurch, Kenley, Northolt, North Weald, Tangmere, Hawkinge and Duxford. All these were in fact sector stations, with the exception of Hawkinge, while Duxford was a sector station of No. 12 Group after some boundary adjustments had taken place that made Debden the station for Sector F, the seventh area added by the time of the Battle of Britain.

During 1937 other changes that took place were the absorption of a further eleven regular squadrons and five squadrons of the Auxiliary Air Force, the latter comprising Nos 600, 601, 604, 607 and 608, although some of these were to fall under the command of No. 12 Group when it moved from Uxbridge, where it had been formed, to Hucknall in May of the same year.

As yet there existed no such thing as a state of preparedness for the squadrons but this was introduced during 1938 at the time of the Munich Crisis and with the exception of the single gap over Christmas 1938, when for a period of ten days the system was suspended, this was continuously maintained from 1938 until 1945.

General mobilization was ordered at 1630 hours on

Friday 1st September 1939, there being nineteen squadrons under the command of the Group at that time. These were: at Tangmere the Hurricanes of Nos 1 and 45 Squadrons, together with the Gloster Gladiators of No. 605 Squadron, Auxiliary Air Force. Another AAF unit, this time equipped with Bristol Blenheim fighters, was No. 600 Squadron at Northolt, where the Hawker Hurricanes of 25 and 111 were also. Northolt had become during those last days of peace something of a showpiece. This had come about because it was situated close to London and because one of that base's machines, flown by the CO Squadron Leader J. W. Gillan, had completed the distance from Edinburgh to home in forty-eight minutes, so that with the aid of a strong following wind an average speed of 408 m.p.h. had been achieved.

The only Spitfires in the Group were all based at Hornchurch in the form of those equipping Nos 54, 65 and 74 Squadrons. There were six remaining regular units in the area, all flying Hurricanes, Nos 17, 56 and 151 at North Weald and Nos 3, 32 and 79 at Biggin Hill. A few days after the outbreak of war, No. 1 Squadron from amongst this number ceased to fall under the control of No. 11 Group when it was sent as part of the Advanced Air Striking Force to France.

The same was true only a short time later of No. 615 Squadron, the Auxiliaries which took their Gloster Gladiators to Merville from Croydon in November 1939 to become part of the Air Component of the BEF. They had moved from their traditional home at Kenley, which was temporarily out of use due to new runways being laid, only a matter of hours before the outbreak of hostilities. There were three further squadrons of the Auxiliary Air Force in No. 11 Group at the time of the mobilization, Hendon-based Nos 601 and 604 with Blenheim fighters and, surprisingly, No. 501, the first Auxiliaries to receive Hawker Hurricanes.

Until the Battle of France there was little of a special

nature to mark the progress of the war for No. 11 Group and almost all of its aerial activity was devoted to standing patrols which had by no means been eliminated with the introduction of RDF and by convoy patrols. There were, however, other now almost forgotten activities such as the protection given to fishing fleets, so that the aircraft became humorously dubbed "Kipper kites", and to lightships, that at one time were targets for Nazi aircraft.

It was following the invasion of the Low Countries that the first major changes took place, although there was a pause after the first reports were received of sections of the Wehrmacht crossing their borders in the early hours of 10th May 1940, until the situation could be accurately assessed. By the 15th, however, the gravity of the events was plain to all and this was emphasized twelve days later when the Belgian surrender was ordered at dawn the next day, so that some of the squadrons in the group were at once placed under the operational control of the AOC of the Air Component in France although they officially remained part of the Group in southern England.

As the situation deteriorated increasing demands were made for further squadrons to be sent to France in an attempt to turn the tide of a battle that was already lost and there followed the period already described when Hugh Dowding was moved to refuse further fighter aid. It was now that the situation arose when some of No. 11 Group's aircraft operated on the Continent, although the French airfields were used as no more than advanced landing grounds. Yet despite these demands convoy and similar patrols were maintained.

A glance at a map will indicate that the great majority of No. 11 Group's airfields were sited south of the Thames and this, it was realized, would automatically impose problems for the fighters operating from them. The reason was due to the fact that, when air operations against Great Britain's south-east corner were begun, the enemy bombers and their escort had the advantage of altitude if the interceptors

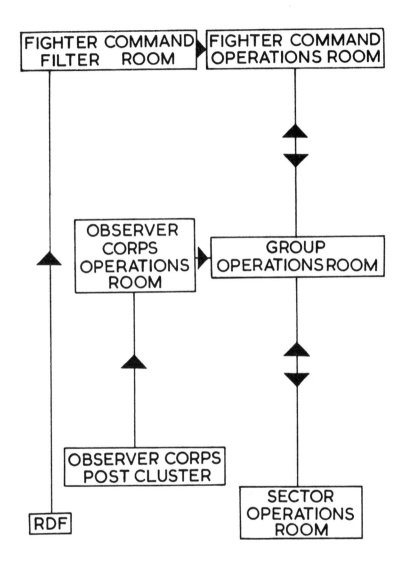

Fighter Command chain of communication

had to be "scrambled" from their base and there were cases of British fighter pilots actually seeing the enemy formations pass over their heads at perhaps 5,000 feet higher when they themselves were still gaining altitude. In fact this happened only rarely since the fighters were not often set to climb in a single direction, using instead a circular course, but it is mentioned to show that the layout of the Group's area was by no means purpose built. It was in fact organized to take the greatest advantage of what was available, and when it came to the choice of airfields this usually meant taking whatever was available, frequently landing grounds that had originally been set up on what open land was to be had in the urban sprawl when the first measures were being taken in the earlier conflict and raiding airships and later bombers had to be intercepted. Even so, the other side of the coin was to the fighters' advantage, for it created a situation that favoured machines returning to their British bases in a damaged condition or perhaps with the pilots wounded as there was no call to pass over the metropolis from, for example, an engagement over the south coast.

Each of the Sectors which fanned out from London came under the control of a Sector Station and these came directly under the command of Group Headquarters at Uxbridge. Identification of these sectors was in alphabetical sequence anti-clockwise from the one at Tangmere which covered such important centres as Southampton and Portsmouth. Last of these in logical sequence was Sector F controlled by Debden, while Sector Z had at its heart the nation's capital.

Immediately above the Group Headquarters in the chain of command came the Command Headquarters at Stanmore, Middlesex. This, like the subordinate centres, had a similar but larger Operations Room that gave a wider picture than those governing the smaller sectors. An interesting sidelight to this introduction is that many officers who were called up when general mobilization was announced were perplexed as to the meaning of the word

"Ops" on their papers since it was a term only just coming into wider usage.

The headquarters of Fighter Command was accommodated in the large building known as Bentley Priory, which took its name from its use before the Reformation by the Austin Canons, it being opened for military use on 14th July 1936. Before this it had been transferred to another brotherhood but was the subject of an exchange between Henry VIII and Cranmer his Archbishop, probably as part of the latter's campaign to do all in his power to retain the favour of the much-married king.

The old building had passed through many hands by 1788 when it was the property of one James Duberly, surprisingly a military uniform manufacturer, who sold it to the Marquis of Abercorn. He was responsible for the erection of the building which would some two hundred years later become Fighter Command Headquarters. The rebuilt house now boasted a picture gallery and was better suited to the lavish entertaining beloved by the Marquis, who had entrusted the redesign to Sir John Soane who made certain that the building would be the jewel in the midst of an enlarged and altered park which was being laid out at the same time. Addington, Pitt and another General who saved his country from a tyrant, the Duke of Wellington, were all among the guests at one time or another.

After other changes of ownership Bentley Priory, now with the addition of a huge conservatory erected by railway engineer John Kelk at a cost of nine thousand pounds, became an hotel, one of a group, Gorden Hotels, owned by Frederick Gorden in the later years of the nineteenth century.

It seemed that there was a curse on the building, said some, for the attempt to use it as an hotel was not a commercial success. Bentley Priory's next role was that of a girls' school, which added soundproofing for music study to some of the rooms and a dozen tennis courts outside.

However, the curse, if one there was, seemed to triumph again in 1924 when the depression of the day meant that the school had to close down in December of that year.

After a period of some months the estate was broken up into two main parts, the larger one being taken over to provide the site of the present housing development, while the smaller part, dominated by the clock tower which had been raised by the builder of the Albert Memorial, Kelk, who had made a present of his work to the nation, was taken over at a cost in the region of £25,000 for use as Inland Area Headquarters of the RAF in May 1926, the move here being later made from Uxbridge.

Ten years were to pass before the alterations that rendered the building to its 1940 state were carried out and the chief feature of these was the conversion of two large rooms for use as an Operations Room and a Filter Room. The latter was where incoming information from the RDF stations was edited for clarity before being fed into the main operations system. This was envisaged only as a temporary measure introduced to gain experience of the new methods, in particular Radiolocation, for it was even now evident that when a European war restarted such a nerve centre would have to be protected underground. Meanwhile, Fighter Command's AOC-in-C Hugh Dowding had ordered that the long trek through the connecting passages be avoided by the cutting of a door to link the pair of vital rooms.

The surface changes that marked the alterations to make the building more properly perform its function of Fighter Command Headquarters were few in number and in the main consisted of the sacrifice of some of the trees and the conservatory. It is somewhat surprising to note that the work on the excavations did not begin until January 1939, so that one wonders just what the position might have been had Great Britain and Nazi Germany gone to war at the time of the Munich crisis, thus bringing a battle for Britain forward perhaps a year.

The work called for the removal of almost 60,000 tons of

earth, some of which was later replaced to cover the series of subterranean rooms that were constructed about the main operations room. Meanwhile other changes which might be noted by the casual observer were the choice by the Commander-in-Chief of a modest room at the back for his personal office, the application of a coat of camouflage paint to the formerly white building and the blacking of the face of the famous time-piece in the ornate tower.

Having looked at the history up to the great testing time of both the nerve-centre of Fighter Command and its subordinate but chief Group, where Air Vice-Marshal Gossage had taken the place of Philip Jourbert in February 1940 before his becoming Inspector General of the RAF, it is necessary at this point to remind ourselves that the sector stations which controlled their own areas about the capital were not the only aerodromes from which the fighters could operate. Indeed had this been so it would have been a simple matter for the enemy to render these useless with a series of concentrated attacks well pressed home. The reason for this not being possible was due to the large number of other stations within the group which were in use either as mere landing grounds or as satellite stations. In the south-eastern corner of England there were many such and all had their part to play during the fateful summer of 1940.

Of these the most westerly was Sector A where Westhampnett acted as a satellite to Tangmere, from which it was separated by only a few miles, the nearest town being perhaps Chichester. It had first come into use as little more than flat meadow-land pressed into service as emergency landing ground with no pretensions to being an aerodrome of any sort, and it was not until the Battle of Britain had actually begun that greater use was made of the area. It was some time later that the first hard runway was constructed and refuelling facilities laid on.

Surprisingly, in the light of its association with all continental air traffic since 1928, Croydon, the former London

Airport of the pre-second World War age, was little more than an extra base attached to Kenley, a station that had been of importance from its early days in 1917 when it was established as the home of No. 7 Aircraft Acceptance Park, where machines were prepared for distribution to the fighting units in France. Perhaps due to its proximity to London, Kenley was regarded as sufficiently important for it to be enlarged some five years before the outbreak of war, although there had been a continuous policy of upgrading so that in the Pilots' Notes for May 1924 we find the warning that special care should be exercised in landing on account of "a large soft patch of ground thirty yards east of the circle . . . this patch being marked with a white cross", while work was reported to be going on in this vicinity some three months later, not being completed until September.

Both these stations, Croydon, following the evacuation of its civil tenants, and Kenley, were similar before the war in that they had only grass runways and although at Kenley hard runways were built by the first days of hostilities, the Gloster Gladiators and Hawker Hurricanes that were the first fighters at the former civil aerodrome were to be operated from grass alone. So were the subsequent Spitfires, which had gone leaving the Hurricane alone by the period of the first attacks on this country. Redhill was a forward aerodrome to Kenley.

A similar situation existed in the neighbouring area of Sector C, where Biggin Hill was the sector station, as might be expected from its long use as a military aerodrome that embraced not only some of the first experiments into night fighting but also early trials with radio as a means of communication with aircraft in flight. In this area the old Maidstone School of Flying had seen the establishment of West Malling as a private field in 1930 and it is interesting to note that it was from here that the Sopwith Dove, which still flies as a Pup during the summer months as part of the Shuttleworth Collection at Old Warden, Bedfordshire, first operated.

By 1934, Malling had become a registered airport although this made only a slight difference to the pattern of the flying from the site and it was not until the beginning of June 1940, just after the last of the British troops had been lifted from the Dunkirk and associated beaches, that the first service units came to the grass runways of the little aerodrome. Sector C also covered Lympne, almost on the south coast, and Detlend, which was poised on the actual boundary dividing it from Sector D to the east.

Command of this area fell to Hornchurch, which owed its beginning to the German air raids on England as long before as 1915 when it had been known by the name that had identified its original use, Sutton's Farm, and BE2c aircraft had been based there as part of the London defence system to the east of the capital. In the opening days of September 1916 the little aerodrome had first leapt into public recognition when it was from here that William Leefe Robinson had taken off to achieve the destruction of the first airship brought down over the British Isles and at the same time win for himself the Victoria Cross.

Another fighter field in the Sector lay north of the Thames Estuary and had a similar history to that of the sector station. This was Rochford, later to be known as Southend, which had also been established as part of the first London defence system against airship raiders and later aeroplanes, it being one of the defenders rising from here that brought down the much publicized *Gotha* in early December 1917; a prize that was not to last long as it was accidentally destroyed by fire before proper examination of its secrets could be made.

After the Armistice in 1918 the area returned to its former agricultural role until 1933 when it was purchased as the site of a municipal airport by the local authority and the opening took place in 1935. It was to be short-lived as a civil aerodrome, however, for two months after the outbreak of the Second World War it again became a service station as a satellite field to Hornchurch.

Across the Estuary to the south lay another satellite, Gravesend, also sometimes known as London East in its civil days, which began in 1932, reputedly following suggestions by Edgar Percival of the aircraft company bearing his name, who would fly here to visit his doctor brother practising in the nearby town.

The first establishment of a service presence was when 1937 found a Reserve Flying School at Gravesend where Naval as well as RAF pilots received instruction. However, the first fighter squadron to make the field its home was No. 32, which arrived with the New Year of 1940, so that the aerodrome henceforth acted as a satellite to Biggin Hill, not the Sector D Station, throughout the Battle of Britain. On 1st March eight years later the site was disposed of as a housing estate and has now largely vanished under bricks and mortar.

With Eastchurch on the Isle of Sheppey two other important fighter fields lay in Sector D: Manston, which was established as nothing more than a group of wooden Naval huts in 1916 and Hawkinge, a part of Lord Radnor's estate when the first aeroplane rose from its grass fully ten years earlier. Manston was another London defence airfield, as its position makes obvious, against the raiders of the earlier conflict but its Naval connections ceased with the creation of the Royal Air Force. Thus began the unbroken association of the site with service flying during the days of the increasingly uneasy peace. Its service use still continues.

Hawkinge was used for ferrying aircraft across the Channel in its first military role and this continued until 1918. It was one year later than an innovation made its appearance at the Channel airfield. This was the introduction of several former DH9 bombers as mail carriers to France, a duty also performed briefly by RAF machines based at Kenley at the time of the Versailles Conference. However, at Hawkinge this too was short-lived and apart from the time when the only fighter squadron earmarked for the defence of the country was based here, it was not until the new Air Defence of Great Britain, the forerunner of Fighter Command, was formed that the station next came into public focus, quite naturally due to its geographical location in the light of the system being geared to attacks from the direction of France.

The first "modern" RAF machines at Hawkinge were Bristol Blenheims but by the time of the historic summer, single-engined fighters ruled supreme, including for a period the ill-fated Defiants with their large drag-producing turrets.

Sector Station of the adjacent E area was North Weald, which had become operational during August 1916, and it was a night interceptor flying from here with Second Lieutenant Tempest at the controls that brought an end to the life of Kapitänleutnant Heinrich Mathy when the airship *L31* was brought down at Potters Bar on the night of 1st October. During the years that followed the end of the war, one of the station commanders was Alfred Guy Garrod, at that time a Wing Commander but destined to be promoted to the rank of Acting Air Marshal by the time of the Battle of Britain as Air Member for Training.

The station continued to act as an RAF base throughout the years that marked "half-time" in the European conflict, and the flamboyant silver and bright metal fighters of the 1930s were common sights here until with seeming suddenness the drab "shadow shading" became permanent with the first monoplane fighters, Hawker Hurricanes of No. 56 Squadron. After the summer of 1940 when the station was heavily bombed, the machines that flew from here continued to be fighters, setting the pattern for the post-war users until 1958 when the station was put on a care and maintenance basis until coming under Army control in 1969 with a consequent appearance of gliders and their winches and gear. In 1979 the old aerodrome was purchased by the local authority.

Closer to the sprawl of north-east London lies Stapleford

Tawney, a satellite of North Weald which was opened in 1934 as a base for Hillman Airways, a well-known charter company of the period, which was later to be merged with two other organizations to form British Airways. After this had taken place flights continued to be carried out from the old base despite Heston being the new centre of operations, a state of affairs that was destined to last for only a few months before Stapleford fell into disuse.

Reawakening came in the form of a new use when RAF flying training began two years later but it was to be the early spring of 1940 before the aerodrome became a fighter station, although in the fullness of time after the sorties in defence of this country, command altered from that by No. 11 Group when the station was absorbed into No. 12.

The flat rather featureless land near to Ipswich makes it an ideal site for an aerodrome so that it was almost inevitable that a portion of this should be taken over a little more than two years after the outbreak of war in 1914. However, it was not to be part of the defences against airships but was intended as a special centre for the testing of aircraft of all types and this was the use to which Martlesham Heath was put from that time until the outbreak of the second conflict when it was succeeded by Boscombe Down. The aerodrome then entered on a new phase as a fighter station, although testing was resumed once more at the end of the decade that had begun with the Battle of Britain, bombing equipment and blind-landing aids for examination being later added to by trials of instruments and armament. Today a part of the site is occupied by the Post Office Research Centre, still dealing with testing but this time of peaceful telecommunications gear.

Sector F boasts both Debden and its satellite, Castle Camps, at one time the base of No. 73 Squadron. The sector station was at one time, before this part of No. 11 Group's boundary was finalized, part of No. 12 Group but Debden was firmly in the area of the metropolitan Group by the time of the opening of the daylight air fighting which took place only three years after the station had been opened as part of the Expansion Scheme, a programme that was often described using the word "panic". Gloster Gladiators and Bristol Blenheims had been its first users but it was Hurricanes that went from here to France soon after the outbreak of war when those of Nos 85 and 87 Squadrons left this airfield, and it is Hurricanes with which the station is largely associated during 1940.

Another strong association that the station has is with the new "Eagle" Squadrons, which were to be the advance guard of the United States Eighth Air Force later in the war before the return of the RAF in the shape of the Gloster Meteors of No. 616 Squadron, to be followed in the post-war years by the RAF Technical College. It was not until as recently as 1975 that the last RAF blue was seen here when the area was handed over to the Army as the site of the new Carver Barracks.

Sundry other RAF stations may be found, all coming under the control of No. 11 Group of Fighter Command, these including such obvious candidates as Hendon, with its strong associations with air displays and royal flying in the days of the 1930s and No. 504 Squadron during the Battle. Another is Ford, in more recent years an open prison but formerly a Fleet Air Arm Station, thus serving as a reminder that fifty-six pilots from the Senior Service fought in the Battle of Britain, nine of them being killed. There is also Deanland near Brighton, but few people now remember it.

Last but by no means least in these thumbnail sketches of No. 11 Group aerodromes must come Northolt, Chief station for Sector Z. This very old station which was opened in March 1915 is said to have been requisitioned a short time before in error when the official held his map the wrong way up! Whatever the truth of the matter there had certainly been an aerodrome of sorts north of the railway line opened by a firm of property speculators in 1912. Apart from its use for London defence, Northolt was later used as a test station by the Fairey Aviation Company and the rather primitive conditions of the day are emphasized by the fact that the RAF's first concrete runways included those laid here in 1936.

After 1940 Transport Command flew from here, although fighters continued to operate until 1944 when Northolt ceased to perform its old role of Sector Station. The transports continued, however, and later included those of the United States Air Force for a time.

When the war was over there began a comparatively short period when the station acted as a civil aerodrome with such aircraft as British European Airways' Dakotas, many of them ex-glider tugs with the towing hook point blanked off, operating to the Channel Islands for instance. However, the RAF was never completely absent and the service presence which still continues was to re-emerge completely with the departure of the civilians in October 1954.

CHAPTER FOUR

The "Ops Rooms"

In the way of life in general and that in the services in particular it was not long before the lengthy term "operations room" was given a less austere and more acceptable ring when it became shortened to "ops room". The idea of a centre of defensive activity was by no means fresh, as control rooms of a similar type had been part of the earlier war.

As already outlined, the nerve centre at the head of Fighter Command was the room at Bentley Priory where alone a complete picture of the whole position was presented. Next came the operations rooms that dealt with the Group-level activities, and similar were the individual rooms that controlled the Sectors, of which there were seven in No. 11's area.

Information gathered by the seaward-looking RDF, as radar was then termed, was fed directly into the main centre at Command Headquarters. However, it arrived in a some-what "rough" state, so much so in fact that to attempt to pass it immediately to the focal point of the centre would have resulted in a glut of information of doubtful value. It was therefore tidied up by being first passed through a Filter Room, where it was subjected to several processes. Perhaps the main one among these was the checking of one set of information against another, while all extraneous information was eliminated, before the edited data was fed into the main Operations Room.

From here the reports, having been presented as "plots" or a series of tracks, identified by number and with relevant information concerning altitude and strength appended, on the operations table with its large-scale map, were passed down the line as it were to the similar rooms (but without filter facilities) at Group level, that for No. 11 being at Uxbridge.

The picture here is the more familiar one, that of a plain room dominated by the central operations table surrounded by plotters standing to move into position the raid plaques with the aid of magnetic rakes in the manner of a croupier. Immediate supervision was exercised by NCOs, both men and women, and above this was a dais with telephones and WAAFs seated in pairs. Communication for the actual plotters was by means of post office "head and breast sets" of the then current pattern with twin headphones and a hinged, horn-like mouthpiece. A single lead from this instrument ran to a standard twin jack under the lip of the table and this ensured that a relieving plotter could plug in her set before the other was extracted, so the position was never vacated even for the brief period of changeover, and faulty instruments could be immediately discovered.

Since the battle was controlled from this room there was a position at a higher level where the Controller and Assistant Controller sat flanked by liaison officers from the Army's anti-aircraft guns and searchlights with those of the Royal Navy and Observer Corps, the service that was to win its spurs in the Battle of Britain and subsequently have "Royal" as part of its name. All these officers were walled off from those at the lower levels by means of a soundproof glass screen and a smaller "theatre box" was provided for visitors. This too was glass-fronted.

About the walls of all operations there was a multitude of wires and conduit neatly clipped into place and in a prominent position was the colour-change clock. This was nothing more than a large-faced time-piece with each fifteen-minute segment divided into three colour periods of five minutes each, red, yellow and blue, so that controllers and supervisors could immediately see the age of the plots laid in the corresponding shade on the horizontal map. Plotters also watched this clock and were expected to remove "stale" plots, although when under pressure this was occasionally overlooked and the cry would go up: "Three colours on the table!" The colour periods could also be picked out by means of a set of automatically altered colour lamps and another innovation introduced at a later date was the colour divisions being doubled in number, so that each was of only two and a half minutes' duration as the speeds of aircraft increased.

Although all operations rooms were basically similar, each had its distinguishing features and one of those at Bentley Priory was the provision of an air-raid warning board, a map of the British Isles including part of Northern Ireland divided into the various warning districts since these did not correspond with Fighter Command Sector divisions. The lowest state of warning exhibited thereon was that known as "Yellow" and this alerted civilian Air Raid Precautions personnel (Civil Defence was a later title), the police and fire brigades. The state indicated that a hostile formation was within twenty minutes' flying time of a locality although not that it was necessarily to be the target. The next step was designated the "Red" warning and was to signal for the public air-raid warning sirens to be sounded to indicate that enemy aircraft were within fifteen minutes of an area. Occasionally this system broke down and bombs were actually falling before the "Alert", as the siren warning was officially called, was sounded. There were even rare cases of this being given after the hostile aircraft had passed, although such a condition should properly have been a "Green" state, when the civilian "Raiders Passed" was given, this being popularly spoken of as "All clear", a legacy from the early bombing raids of just over twenty years before.

But if the Operations Room at Fighter Command had this unusual feature there was one that it shared with that at Group level, namely a display indicating the state of the fighter squadrons operating in each sector. This took the form of lists headed with the squadron number displayed under the appropriate Sector name: Tangmere, North Weald, Hornchurch and so on, and below the various categories of preparedness or action. These were fourteen in number, the first ten being divided by coloured bands from those which showed likely interception and were as follows: Released, Available twenty minutes, Available, Ordered to Readiness, At Readiness (five minutes), Ordered to Standby, At Standby (two minutes), Ordered on Patrol, Left Ground, In Position; and the final, vital four: Detailed to Raid, Enemy Sighted, Ordered to Land, with finally Landed and Refuelling, the operative condition being shown by rows of lamps beneath each heading. A further series of indicators below these lists showed the heights at which various sections of the balloon barrage were flying over London, Gravesend and thereabouts, while the space between these boards gave weather information and accommodated a blackboard for the record of raid numbers, aircraft type and units involved, amongst other information. It was a Group's responsibility to keep this information up to date at Command level, so two-way communication was called for between these levels.

Fed into the Group Ops Room also was the data collected

from the Observer Corps Centres, each of which had its own room of a similar type to those of the RAF. This was supplied by two-man crews of the observer posts, which might be sited in any of a wide variety of locations from the tops of town buildings to mere sand-bagged emplacements in the open country. Three or occasionally four of these Posts were joined to form a Cluster, identified by a letter that also served as a prefix to the Post number, always a single digit, so that there was both "Able One" and "Baker One", and so on, in the phonetic alphabet of the day.

At these the Post observers had divided duties. One, wearing a head and breast set, would operate the Post Instrument, popularly known later as the Micklethwait, a device that gave the position of a sighted aircraft or formation on a small circular section of the immediate area that duplicated a similar portion of the Main Table at the local ops room. Like its larger version it was covered by the superimposed lines of the British Modified Grid, a system that gave square rather than rectangular divisions, unlike the grid that replaced the earlier one in the early 1950s. This gave the exact position by a series of reference numbers which could be told to the Centre plotter together with the height of the raid, direction and identification of the aircraft type, this latter being the duty of the second man equipped with binoculars. This at least was the official arrangement but as will be seen it placed much responsibility on the single operator and gave somewhat light duties to his fellow so that, some said, he could brew the tea! In practice a better balance of work was usually arrived at, and rightly so for, despite the often repeated remarks that a post instrument was a Heath Robinson type of device, it in fact called for a skilled man to operate it correctly if full use was to be made of its potential.

General arrangement of the Observer Corps centres, of which there were seven covering the area of No. 11 Group and its periphery, at Maidstone, Colchester, Winchester,

Sectors of No. 11 Group

Oxford, Watford, Horsham and Bromley, was very similar to that in the RAF rooms. The same system of Grid divisions, colour phases and dais arrangement was used. There was, however, an important difference, quite apart from the obvious one that the seated plotters used no magnetic rakes, their table being less large: this was the employment of a Long Range Board, a large vertical map with the Observer Corps Group area in its midst drawn to a smaller scale so that surrounding groups' tracks and plots over the sea could be recorded.

Back in the RAF Fighter Command system, this information obtained via the highly competent personnel of the Observer Corps, whose responsibilities went far beyond the mere identification of sundry aircraft as is often believed, was absorbed into the group picture and with the remainder of the information passed to the Sector Operations Rooms where the actual control of the intercepting fighters was undertaken.

These Sector rooms were at first envisaged as being solely located on the aerodrome that was the centre of each sub-division, and these were of two types. That planned before ten years of the Expansion Scheme of the late 1930s consisted of bungalow-type buildings with a conventional pitched roof, the only protection being offered by the erection of a high bank of earth about the outer walls rising to approximately the height of the gutters. It was soon appreciated that buildings such as these could very simply be knocked out by an attack on the Sector Station, a fact hardly surprising when it is realized that these were mere legacies of the former Air Defence of Great Britain which did not envisage an attack coming from the old enemy.

However, although it was appreciated that all would not be well in these, there was insufficient time to do much about it but better things were hoped for on those of the new type associated with the developments that followed the creation of the new command. It was now that when new operations rooms were put up they were planned along different lines, the buildings themselves being shaped after the manner of a capital L, thus at once ensuring a minimization of blast damage and a stronger structure. However, due to the shortage of time available only three such were erected in No. 11 Group, at Hornchurch, Tangmere and North Weald. Unfortunately all were to spring up in the fashion of the older models, namely on the aerodromes themselves, so that they suffered the same disadvantage of providing ideal targets. That this was realized in official circles is indicated by the fact that there was a rush to find alternative operations rooms. These were all somewhat rough and ready but were not on the Sector Station, being housed in a variety of buildings which were not recognizable.

Typical of these were those intended to control the Kenley sector, which was among those having one of the older-style bungalow buildings, and as an alternative a redundant butcher's shop was used in nearby Caterham Valley. The work of preparing this was carried on, if not exactly in secret, then in something of a low key and one of the first changes was to erect new internal walls that also had the result of preventing the inquisitive from seeing what was going on. Less well known is that, as in many cases, there was a second emergency room, this one being accommodated in a large mansion standing a short distance away, although in the case of Kenley the centre did not come into use until after 1940.

Nevertheless these are mentioned to show the type of building that came into use. There were also others: school and church halls, large houses and even garages were all pressed into service, that for Sector "C" illustrating the wisdom of these makeshift rooms being set up; for, although there was a temporary centre established in a shop about three quarters of a mile distant, the use of another large mansion some way off made all the difference when the Operations room at Biggin Hill aerodrome, sited on the periphery of the station proper, received a direct hit on 31st August.

The duties of these vital rooms in the chain of command was quite simple; while the Fighter Command Room at Bentley Priory kept abreast of the countrywide position, the responsibility for the decision when a "hostile" was to be intercepted rested with the commanders at group level, so that all the actions which were fought over the area of No. 11 were initiated at Uxbridge. The actual order to scramble came slightly further down the chain, for this came from the sector and henceforth the fighters were under the direction of the Sector Controller, although the final link in the chain, that forged by the formation or flight leader, was the source of the actual decision to attack.

Until recently it would have been believed that an account of the information sources concerning the enemy's intentions had been exhausted by a detailed description such as the foregoing, but we now know that such is not the case, although the secret has been kept for more than thirty years, and even today the full story is not available.

The fact of the matter is that thanks to the success with which the Nazi codes had been broken by cryptanalysis, the Air Officer Commanding-in-Chief at Fighter Command had a prior knowledge of the Luftwaffe's plans: this was the "secret intelligence sources" which were vaguely indicated only a year after the end of the war. The communications code was known as Enigma and its breaking as Ultra.

At this point Stanmore once again figures in our narrative for it was here that one of the Special Liaison Units, usually referred to as SLUs, was set up just in time to be of service at the height of the battle in August. This was for the express information of Hugh Dowding. Despite the still incomplete picture, it is known that when Luftflotte 5 was preparing an attack from the north, flying from its Scandinavian bases on 15th August, it was possible for Leigh-Mallory's No. 12 Group and the neighbouring No. 13 to be warned in advance.

The value of such advance warning is demonstrated by reference to the second attack mounted on 15th September, later regarded as Battle of Britain Day, when three waves of Heinkels and Dorniers drawn from KG2, KG53 and KG76 were flung against London under the protection of a strong escort of single-seat fighters found by JG26 and JG54—two very experienced units.

It was only a little after 2 p.m. when the huge formation, so big in fact that ten miles of sky were needed to accommodate its width, appeared over London's outer defences in Kent, only to be set upon by a little under two hundred Spitfires and Hurricanes and a fierce engagement ensued. The fighting was of such intensity that the Nazi aircrews were astonished and despite their orders that the raid was to be pushed home with the maximum of effort were only too ready to rid themselves of their bomb loads over the fringes of London so that they fell on such areas as Catford, East Ham, Ladywell and Crofton Park in addition to others. They then altered course for France as soon as possible, all the while still being harried by defenders who had the advantage of position and height from the outset. This was as much a victory for the Ultra system as for No. 11 Group, and one which would not have been so resoundingly successful had the codebreakers done their work less thoroughly. The intercepted message was passed direct to Dowding and from him to Keith Park, the distribution having an unexpectedly everyday look consisting as it did of single sheets of paper, marked in common with a vast quantity of typescript of the period "Most Secret". Being ordinary and for the most part double-spaced sheets clearing that the information had come from a "reliable source", they excited little comment and only a very few realized that the vital intelligence had come from the code-named Ultra machine.

There were undoubtedly other instances of the advance information via this source being used to the advantage of Fighter Command by the simple expedient of listening to the radio messages and feeding them into the code-breaking machine, a state of affairs made the more easy by the fact that although the Luftwaffe was one of the most intense users of wireless they continued to do so in complete ignorance that the code had been broken. In fact the use of code at all was a reversion to a more military method of communication since in the preceding spring it had not been uncommon for many Wehrmacht units to discard any pretence of secrecy so high was morale and their confidence in victory, sending radio messages in clear.

It should be stated that the long lapse of time which has passed before the release of the Ultra secret is in large measure due to the personal integrity of Hugh Dowding, who refused to divulge what the "reliable sources" of information were, even in his own defence when certain factions made him the victim of a witch-hunt to reap personal gain.

The subject of communications and their inter-relation with intelligence brings us to the first association of this branch of service work with the men in the cockpits and it is perhaps best first to look into the method of estimating combat victory claims.

These assessments really fell into two distinct periods of time, a fact not always realized but regrettably true since it must reopen the question of the losses claimed by each side both at the time and subsequently and which, if any, are completely accurate. However that may be, the first period for the analysis of combat claims was that which existed between the earliest days of the aerial engagements until August and this awarded only two categories. In the first of these it was necessary for an enemy aircraft to have been seen either going down on fire with visible flames: smoke was not sufficient. Alternatively the foe must have been seen to disintegrate in flight. All this had additionally to have taken place under the gaze of independent witnesses, be they either other members of the intercepting formation or perhaps watchers on vessels or coastguards. An alternative to a confirmed "kill" such as these were the unconfirmed losses, when the enemy machine must have been observed to have been forced to break off combat "in circumstances that led the [British] pilot to believe that it would have been a loss".

As the Battle of Britain reached its summit and greater experience was gained it was realized that a wider method of grading enemy losses was desirable, although as already indicated the change has left historians with two irreconcilable sets of results. Under the new categories there were to be three grades: damaged, probably destroyed and destroyed. For listing under the final heading the assessment was virtually unchanged from the first method: that is, an enemy machine must have been seen to break up in the air, fall in flames or crash either on land or into the sea. The "probably destroyed" group was now much the same as that which had formerly been termed an unconfirmed loss, so that the new grouping was in practice confined to that known as damaged and for this it was demanded that parts of the enemy machine be seen to come away, undercarriages drop down or other severe and visible harm to be inflicted. Perhaps enough has been said here to show that the attempts to compare the claims of machines lost by both sides can never be reconciled. The pursuit of such matters must for ever remain hopeless since there must have been a vast array of circumstances in which machines believed in the heat of combat to have been "probably destroyed" had in fact managed to limp home despite the seeming gravity of their condition. On the other hand there will have been those machines, particularly single-seaters, where the damage which seemed to be fairly trivial was in fact more serious than could be made out from another aircraft where the pilot was fighting for his own life anyway and his opponent was to find a grave in the numbing cold of the Channel out of sight of any other human being. The German and British attitudes to the surrounding sea were markedly different, for while the Britisher tends to regard the English Channel as a fairly friendly expanse of water, the Luftwaffe crews did not share this viewpoint.

Factors such as these would have been taken into account by the more astute intelligence officers attached to Fighter Command, for the assessment of the enemy position could at times be based only on their judgement of the situation, the publishing of claims of losses for civilian consumption being only a small part of their work.

The intelligence service of Fighter Command was therefore a vital part of the organization and the estimates made by those of No. 11 Group during the summer of 1940 were doubly so.

First beginnings of the organization had really taken place in 1938 when in a letter of 21st April the Air Council had asked the Commander in Chief of Fighter Command for more detailed suggestions concerning the method of establishing such a branch and what the duties might be in modern warfare. To this end a letter was prepared under the date of 6th May by Squadron Leader Norwood, the Command Intelligence Officer, although this document had first been personally amended by Dowding himself, and the final classification was seen to fall under three distinct headings, those of Command, Group and Station Intelligence.

Of these the first was seen to have somewhat differing responsibilities in peace and in war and in the latter the work was in the main that of acting as a supply source to Groups and stations of information required to carry out their own duties as outlined later, obtaining much of this from the Air Ministry, the MOD (Air) of the day.

In time of war, however, the letter presented in the form of a Memorandum foresaw that the Intelligence staff of the Command would also have to draw on a wide spectrum of additional sources of information. There would be not only the immediately obvious ones at lower level with which a two-way exchange would be maintained, but also the anti-aircraft and searchlights, other Commands of the RAF, principally Coastal and Bomber, and including Balloon and the Observer Corps. All these would have been in direct communication but there were also those with which liaison would be maintained via the Air Ministry: the ARP organization, the War Office (now MoD, Army) and the Admiralty. These were not the only sources envisaged, for it was foreseen that within the duties of the Command Intelligence Organization would fall the interrogation of captive aircrew, the examination of books, documents, maps and plans which fell into British hands and also an investigation of captured aircraft.

From all these it would be possible to assess the strength, morale and general disposition of enemy air forces and to maintain an enemy Order of Battle plus the preparation of Intelligence Summaries and their distribution.

It was therefore foreseen in 1938 that the officers appointed would have to possess a very complete knowledge, not only of their own organization but also of the enemy and the various branches of Home Defence.

Intelligence duties at Group level would have been very similar to those already outlined but the liaison would be a two-way traffic to higher level and also downwards to those of the stations and to brief Operations Staff. The officers responsible here, it was judged, would have to perform very similar duties to those already outlined, but their proximity to the actual fighting would also entail their ensuring that pilots were kept abreast of changes in enemy equipment, armament, characteristics, markings and so on, as well as perform the well-known function of interrogating the pilots and forming a balanced judgement of their observations and claims.

Squadron Leader Norwood's original report further suggested that Command Headquarters would also be the best posting for specialist interpreters, but in the event the recommendation was not carried out and instead the work was actually carried out at station level by a special group known as AI1(K) in conjunction with another, AI1(G), although these designations were later to be changed. The operations of these groups were confined to specified but adjacent areas throughout Fighter Command and would embrace both the interrogation of prisoners and the examination of aircraft brought down. These specialist officers were seen as having to possess a wide knowledge of the Luftwaffe's organization and workings, coupled with a fluent command of German. Even so, it remained the responsibility of the station intelligence staff to work in conjunction with the AI1(K) and AI1(G) sections and to supervise the proper guarding of prisoners and to take into British official custody documents and the like discovered on crews or within a wreck.

At this point the name of Keith Park reappears since at the beginning of 1939 he had not yet taken command of No. 11 Group but was acting as Group Captain, Operations, to the Senior Air Staff Officer with the rank of Air Commodore. It was to him that the Norwood suggestions were passed with the footnote admitting that some modifications would undoubtedly have to be incorporated in the light of experience. With this Park agreed and after the addition of some minor details, the document was passed back to the intelligence section for the requisite action to be taken bearing the comment that it was "a most useful paper".

Creating Fighter Command's new Intelligence organization, which was to be so fully exercised during the hectic days marking the summer of 1940, naturally brought with it the problem of the calibre of manpower that was to supply the necessary personnel, and official records exist to suggest that the founders were staff drawn from the Command Education Service in the autumn of 1938. The formation of this nucleus was nothing if not timely for it was that same September which saw the Nazi seizure of Austria. With the developing situation now clear for all to see the creation of further Fighter Command Groups north of the original boundaries of No. 11's area took place as speedily as possible and this naturally had the effect of increasing the demand for the necessary manpower. To meet this, four likely sources were named in a letter from the Directorate of Intelligence to Hugh Dowding, these being: regular RAF personnel, former RAF members on the retired and Reserve List, the Royal Air Force Volunteer Reserve and members of the Civil (Staff Duty) List, and it was anticipated that the nominations from the first three groups would come from the Air Ministry direct. Age ranges for the final group were defined as being between thirty-two and fifty, although it was realized that this might debar some with very specialized knowledge, so it was stated that a flexible interpretation of these categories would be practised. In the main those selected would be linguists.

There were only five days of peace left to run when No. 11 Group Headquarters was informed by the Air Ministry that to fill the Flight Lieutenant vacancies in the Command as a whole fifteen appointments had been made, to be distributed amongst the Central Group and the two others then in existence; they had all been commissioned direct into the RAF Volunteer Reserve from civil life.

The basis of Fighter Command Intelligence had by all this been most carefully laid, not only through the painstaking work of Squadron Leader Norwood but also by the Commander-in-Chief, another facet of the little-known work that Hugh Dowding contributed in the short days of careful planning that brought victory a small step nearer in the coming fight for survival; for the work was vital and all could have been rendered as nought if the formative months had been wasted or wrongly used. The work performed by Intelligence Officers was very frequently mundane and never spectacular, always being surrounded in secrecy, but if "know your enemy" is a truthful maxim then these men ensured that the defenders of these islands did just that.

Part Two

CHAPTER FIVE

Pause Before Battle

British troops were still coming home from France at the beginning of June but there was no doubt in anyone's mind now that all was lost and it was thought to be only a very short time before the grey hordes that were engulfing Europe would be poised for an assault across the English Channel. The Nazi High Command believed that the British Army had no more than twenty fully trained and equipped divisions but that in the air the RAF was still relatively strong due to the intense pre-war preparations, an image that may have been partly owing to a deliberate attempt to foster this idea, the measures even including organized visits for Nazi officers to view British "shadow factories"—a term commonly used at the time for those works producing military aircraft.

The real position, as later revealed in official documents, was that Fighter Command had some fifty squadrons considered fit for operations and of these about half were located in No. 11 Group, twelve of them equipped with Hawker Hurricanes, two with Bristol Blenheim night fighters and the remainder flying Spitfires, although the Orders of Battle would have shown slightly different returns a little later since the sectors of Filton and Middle Wallop then in the group were about to be transferred to the command of No. 10 Group in the middle of July.*

Opposing the defenders in northern France were about 1,500 aircraft, two thirds of them bombers. That this presented a grim picture was obvious but the position was in reality worse since these numbers did not represent the entire Nazi air strength in western Europe, for it was reckoned that between Amsterdam and Brest was poised another force consisting of 1,500 long-range bombers, 500 dive-bombers and 1,000 Messerschmitt 109 and 110 fighters.

As far as was known there was no time in which to expand Britain's fighter force—the chances of this had long passed—but even were this not the case the operations over France as that country fought and lost its last battle had made serious demands on British resources. The beginning of June found a pressing need for a period of re-equipment and reorganization before further expansion could be contemplated, a fact which explains why during the three months from July to September inclusive only four new units were added to Fighter Command, two Polish, one Czech and one Canadian. Pilot strength was 1,253, a deficiency of 197 below the established figure.

In the sphere of hardware not all Fighter Command's aircraft were fitted with self-sealing tanks nor fitted with armour, neither were all fitted with constant speed airscrews, IFF (Identification Friend or Foe)—the electronic device that marked an aircraft as "friendly" on the radio location (RDF) screens—or even rear-view mirrors. The

* At 12 o'clock, noon, on Thursday, 18th July.

first deficiency was remedied by teams of fitters travelling round the Command to make the necessary modifications, while the last was made good by squadron personnel who brought a brisk trade to such suppliers as Halfords who dealt in motor accessories!

On the international front the picture offered Great Britain few rays of hope. Paris had been bombed with a loss of 290 lives, it was announced on 4th June, and ten days later the city was to fall, an event captured by the nation's crooners a brief while later in the popular song of the time "The last time I saw Paris". Meanwhile Italy's Fascist dictator, Benito Mussolini, a former journalist with political ambitions like many before and since, had declared war on the Allies.

So far there had been little Nazi air activity over Great Britain and the country existed in a strange state that was neither peace nor total war, with such luxuries as imported fruit in the shops, past which civilians went with official cardboard boxes containing their gas masks suspended over one shoulder on a string. The newspapers and news bulletins meanwhile announced that in the middle of the month a second British Expeditionary Force had embarked for France; five days later they were home again in luckier circumstances than their earlier colleagues since most of their equipment also returned intact, or so it was reported. At about this time also the United States declared that all material aid would be given to the Allies, although this cheered few at the time since with the best will in the world nothing could remedy the immediate situation.

Still the Luftwaffe waited and such appearances as it made over British shores were mainly confined to reconnaissance near the coastal areas. Although the districts covered were mainly far away from where the coming battle was to take place, such as Aberdeenshire, the Firth of Tay, Tyneside, the Bristol Channel, the Firth of Forth, Devon, Dorset and the estuary of the Humber, Dover was also visited. Here the concentration of ships in the harbour that had seemed to provide an ideal target just before the turn of the month was ignored, although there was a small attack on shipping off the South Foreland about this time when four bombs were dropped. Meanwhile the work continued in Dover's mortuary in Tower Street to clear the backlog of over two hundred corpses that had been brought ashore, and burials not only of British soldiers but also of Frenchmen and Belgians took place almost daily in St James' Cemetery. Had the Nazis sent their bombers across the Channel at this time, or at least opened the coming attacks with concentrated assaults on British airfields, the final outcome might have been different but in fact nothing of this nature was attempted until much later in the summer.

It was as the month of June advanced that the earliest intrusions into the everyday life of civilians were really made by the war situation when the first "defence areas" were established; twenty-mile-wide belts spreading inland from the coast from a point beginning at the Wash and terminating on the eastern border of Sussex near to Rye. It was officially announced that "It is not a closed area and there is no desire to interfere with journeys for business or other important reasons". Six days later the position was clarified when the area was extended about the northern shore of the Wash into Lincoln and the news media stated that Regional Civil Defence Commissioners would have the power to control all people entering the area. At much the same time barrage balloons began to appear flown from even public parks in the centre of London where armed sentries often in full battle order stood guard on government buildings and measures were introduced to "set the sea on fire" by igniting thousands of gallons of petroleum spirit floating on the surface of the Channel, that area off Dover in the region of St Margaret's Bay being set alight with the aid of a Westland Lysander retained in the vicinity and bombed up with incendiaries.

As the month approached its mid-point there was a small

increase in aerial activity on both sides, as for instance the attack that was launched on the night of Wednesday 19th June, raids later to be described as "the greatest air attack of the war". Not all of these were confined to the area controlled by No. 11 Group, being spread from the east coast of Scotland and Yorkshire, southwards through County Durham and Lincolnshire to the south-east coast. The bombers were seemingly taking advantage of the bright moonlight conditions, for all the raiders appeared after the fall of darkness.

The policy of quoting place names of targets bombed was not adhered to on this occasion for one incident that was widely reported was when a bomb from one of the raiders reported to have been more than a hundred in number fractured a pipeline on a wharf carrying oil at Thames Haven. At one moment there was the complete blackness that the wartime ban on external lights imposed, and then with a piercing whistle later to become familiar but at that time new and alarming, there was a sudden explosion that sent up a gush of flame that settled quickly into the leaping inferno with its billowing cloud of black smoke that the burning contents of the pipe gave. Soon the bells were going down as the London Fire Brigade sent appliances to converge on the spot taking some of the men, their traditional helmets replaced by steel ones of military pattern, to fight their first oil fire.

On the following Thursday Fighter Command claimed that seven of the raiders had been brought down, and the end of one Heinkel 111 bomber was well publicized when it fell to the guns of a Blenheim of No. 604 Squadron that had just moved to Northolt from Manston, flying the type they had taken on strength the previous April. These machines were former bombers converted to fighters with the addition of a quartet of forward-firing machine guns in a tray under the fuselage, a modification produced in the workshops of the Southern Railway Company.

Tried earlier as a day fighter, the Blenheim had proved

unequal to the task and had been relegated to patrols under cover of darkness. For these the twin-motor Bristol products were fitted with what at the time was usually referred to in RAF circles as "magic mirrors". They were in fact the first carriers of AI, an early airborne type of "radiolocation", by means of which a target was located with the aid of a forward-projected radio signal with its reflection registered on a cathode-ray tube, all relatively new since it had proved difficult to compress the new Radiolocation with its heavy equipment into sets capable of fitting within the restrictions of an aeroplane, although at this stage AI was far from reliable.

Another pilot, "sailor" Malan in fact, claimed that two Heinkels fell to his guns at fifty yards' range a little before 1 a.m. both over the Thames Estuary, but it was another which was fired at and seemed to escape that provided the story of the night. Shortly before dawn a Heinkel was seen to be losing height over the coast as the pilot set course over the sea. Although both engines were still running one of them was emitting a strange note and in the half light flames and a streak of black oily smoke could be seen coming from the motor. It was flying at an altitude of no more than thirty feet as it crossed the shingle and was obviously doomed, so it was no surprise to the watchers on the shore when the bomber ploughed into the waves some distance out sending up a great wash of leaping water as it did so. For a moment there was no movement from the wreck. "They're all gonners!" someone shouted as the aircraft seemed to settle into the salt water. Then a spectator detected a movement, followed by another, and soon four figures could be made out trying to launch a rubber dinghy. Before they had accomplished this there was the crunch of running feet on the pebbles as a group of armed coastguards appeared.

As their life-raft finally ran aground in the shallow water the four crewmen waded the last few yards, their flying suits made heavier by the weight of water. An airman fumbled towards the hip of his trousers and one of the coastguards, all auxiliary men, cocked his own weapon suspecting that the Nazi was reaching for a revolver. At this the airmen took the precaution of raising their hands in the air and after they had been motioned to stand still while they were searched they were marched off to captivity by the group which had now been joined by a policeman.

The activities of this night, which included some attacks on RAF aerodromes—"without success", said official communiqués—were summed up by Nazi radio in the following terms: "German air formations bombed numerous air bases in England as well as the great oil storage tanks at the mouth of the Thames, which were set on fire."

On the other side of the coin June 1940 was also the time when there was an increased awareness of the work of the Royal Air Force's Bomber Command, although it had been bringing the air war to the heart of enemy territory since before the Battle of France, and if a balanced picture of the Battle of Britain is to be painted it must be realized that the contribution to victory was made as much by the service as a whole as by Fighter Command alone. It was just that the work of the latter was carried on by daylight under the full gaze of the public and the awareness that something positive and practical was being done appealed to the public's imagination at the time.

Typical of the raids against targets in Nazi Germany was that mounted during June against an oil refinery near Hanover in which, so popular rumour had it, Hermann Göring had business interests. It was against this that a force of bombers from No. 83 Squadron was sent from Scampton, flying "Panhandles", otherwise Handley Page Hampdens, the peculiar twin-engined bombers of the time that were distinguished by their heavy-looking front fuselages and narrow, high-set cockpits. The raid was organized to take place in the third week of the month when the moon was approaching its full point, so all below stood out sharply lit as the first wave of the bombers came in at about

15,000 feet. Their 500-pound bombs seemed to do immediate damage since it was not long before some of the buildings were seen to be well alight and glowing with a dull, cherry-red luminosity. The final stroke was delivered by a pair of machines that had been waiting at a higher level. They now came down to an extremely low altitude, only a little more than 300 feet, before the bomb-aimers released their loads and from the great gushes of flame that immediately erupted it was assumed that direct hits had been scored. One of the pilots on this occasion was Flying Officer Guy Gibson, better known later as a Wing Commander and holder of the Victoria Cross.

June was distinguished by something like twenty sorties and for No. 83 Squadron attacks against industrial targets provided a welcome change from the earlier mine-laying missions, known as "gardening", since before this the strict limitations on the type of centre that might be attacked made the work irksome and lacking in variety.

The evening of 19th June was not only the one on which the Luftwaffe delivered its heaviest attack to date, causing the British newspapers the following morning to run such headlines as "Mass Bombing Begins", adding that in their Cambridgeshire homes nine, including several children, had perished. The RAF too had taken advantage of the near-full moon to deliver an attack on the Rhineland, the Ruhr valley and other parts of north-west Germany. It was claimed that 250 bombs of various calibres had been dropped on Bremen in the space of ten minutes, causing fires among the oil storage tanks. The previous night Castrop, Düsseldorf, Sterkrade, Essen, Hanover, Cologne, Hamburg and Frankfurt had all been bombed, the targets including the power stations and railway marshalling yards, in addition to petrol refineries and oil storage tanks, the latter mainly at Misburg. It was claimed at the time that the heavy anti-aircraft fire had accounted for only three of the attackers and it is certainly true that a large number of intelligence reports have survived, many of these making special mention of the spectacular results of bombing the power stations, for these took the form of vivid flashes of blue-white zigzag light that settled down into sullen glows of fire that could still be observed at altitude from a distance of eighty miles. Some of these raids were carried out from an extremely low level, perhaps to compensate for the small numbers of aircraft that could be sent, for we now know that it was possible to order only about six machines to each target, although the news media made much of the weight of the attacks without of course divulging the number of bombers used. However, all was felt to be worth the expenditure of lives and aircraft, since the basic philosophy was still to frustrate the invasion attempts that were seen as almost unavoidable, hence the concentration on Nazi rail centres and oil supplies, all of which would have been vital in an attempted assault on the fortress that was the Great Britain of 1940.

On one of these occasions when No. 83 Squadron had detailed only four machines to attack targets in Gelsen-kirchen, three other Hampdens were sent to bomb Soest, the main targets being the signal boxes which controlled a large network of lines over which troop-trains might pass. The bombers on the latter mission were following the course of the River Ruhr at an altitude of no more than 500 feet, the pilots with their canopies open in the manner of a single-seat aircraft to aid course-keeping. Turning to star-board the formation had no difficulty in picking out the shimmering expanse of the Mohne Lake, of later historical note, as it lay like a mirror in the moonlight. A few miles to the north was the target.

As the pilots pulled the aircraft up to about 600 feet before commencing the bombing run the fire from the ground batteries became fiercer, one aircraft suffering damage to a wing-tip so that with bombs gone the pilot sought the safety of a lower height, only to have a shell splinter sever the control cables to the twin rudders. At the moment when this happened the machine was still in a dive and recovery with elevators and ailerons proved to be quite a problem. Just as this appeared to be possible provided there was plenty of space to manoeuvre, one of the tall houses which are so common in central Europe seemed to loom out of the darkness of the summer night as the Hampden straightened up over a road junction.

With the aircraft now flying straight and level once more the pilot had a chance to take stock of the situation and he at once realized that the shell splinters had done more damage than he had at first thought, for one had struck the port engine with the result that the oil pressure had dropped below danger level. Despite this the Hampden was able to limp home although for the whole journey the crew were conscious of the fact that should the motor, starved of lubricant, finally seize up they were at too low a height to do anything more than rely on the skill of the pilot to get them down, since their altitude was insufficient for parachutes to be used. Less fortunate was the crew of another machine that crashed killing all on board at Scampton. It was later discovered that the pilot had been wounded over the target and was not able to control the machine properly for landing, the peculiar arrangement of the Hampden making it impossible for the controls to be handed over in flight.

Another target which came in for attention at this time was the large Dornier factory at Wismar on the Baltic coast. At the time the products delivered from here were mainly bombers and it was realized that these machines would be required in large numbers to destroy British aerodromes as a preliminary to invasion. Squadrons 49 and 83, both flying Hampdens and based at Scampton, were detailed to this raid and although in the event the former failed to find the target, the other squadron was successful and, despite the heavy anti-aircraft fire, managed to drop their bombs in the manner of all such raids at this period, that is to say from a low altitude, since the small numbers of aircraft that could be detailed to a target had to be compensated for by making every bomb tell.

At the same time, public opinion was far more appreciative of the true role of such sorties than in later periods. Such raids as those that have been briefly described were looked upon as part of the broader picture of the RAF's work, and people realized that it was raids such as these as well as the achievements of Fighter Command that frustrated the Nazi hopes of invading the British Isles. Most people in 1940 assumed that this was inevitable so that the bombing of the slowly accumulating groups of invasion barges that were among the other targets attacked were all seen as contributions not to taking the war into the enemy territory but as part of the broader issue of the defence of the realm. The belief that invasion was inevitable in the minds of many is shown by the number of private arrangements that people made for the reunification of their families after the tide of battle had passed and a typical one was that made by Ronald Adam, before and later well known as an actor but then a Squadron Leader working in the Operations Room of the Sector Station at Hornchurch. His girlfriend at the time was a pretty little NCO in the Women's Auxiliary Air Force named Allyne Franks, later to be promoted to Section Officer and thus become the first WAAF to receive a commission from Hornchurch, and still later to become Mrs Adam. The couple agreed that if the invasion of Great Britain parted them then one or other would attempt to make it known that they had survived. Since the aftermath of invasion would find the country with no communications system some other means had to be found. To this end the couple recalled that in the cloisters of Canterbury Cathedral, one of Ronald's favourites, was the tomb of Archbishop Davidson. Here, they decided, would be an ideal place for one of them to leave a message in the hope that the other would find it and in that way the two would be able to find one another again.

While private arrangements such as these were being made there were measures being taken at every level to repel the troops in field-grey who had already marched in triumph through the French capital itself and might soon be parading in the Strand in London. An extra impetus was therefore given to the now largely forgotten work of those behind the scenes at such centres as Farnborough in Hampshire where the enemy's secrets were probed. These findings were no less a contribution to victory than the seemingly unending sorties flown a few weeks later by the operational pilots who had on occasion to be lifted from their cockpits sound asleep after executing near perfect landings and shutting off the engines; as the adrenalin had ceased to flow, weariness had overtaken them and they had merely succumbed to fatigue.

It is now necessary for us to turn our attention back in time to the Battle of France and the last months of 1939. By now there had been set up at Orléans Bricy a Test Centre for Flying Material, in other words an establishment where captured aircraft might be examined, be they complete machines or mere parts salvaged from wrecks. Among the former, as the first year of the war drew to a close, were two complete Messerschmitt 109E fighters, the suffix causing the type to be dubbed "Emils" in the Luftwaffe. Of these, one was soon lost in a crash suffered during part of a flight test programme, but the survivor was a machine formerly belonging to the second Gruppe of Jagdgeschwader 54, otherwise known as the Grünhertz, as shown by their emblem usually carried on the starboard side of their fighters' fuselages, a green heart.

The specimen in question was in fact an Me 109E-3* and it was flown to Boscombe Down by Flying Officer M. H. Brown of No. 1 Squadron early in 1940 before being passed on to the Royal Aircraft Establishment at Farnborough on 14th May. It was here that test flying really began in earnest, using the precious example, number 1304, to compare with British fighters, throughout the remainder of May and into the vital breathing space that June was providing.

* Strictly, Bf 109 is more correct but the popular and more readily understood "Me" of the time is used here.

In order to extract the last ounce of comparable data from the machine a formidable team of the most able and experienced British fighter pilots was assembled to fly the type and this included such illustrious names as that of (then) Flight Lieutenant Bob Stanford Tuck of 92 Squadron and Wing Commander George Stainforth, who had set up a new World Air Speed Record of 407.5 miles per hour nine years before in the Spitfire's predecessor, the Schneider Trophy-winning Supermarine S6B. The third member of the test team was Flying Officer J. E. Peabody.

When work such as this is undertaken it is not enough to discover how an enemy machine responds in combat alone: it is necessary to know everything about a type in order that its good points may be known as much as its weak ones. One of the first phases of the tests therefore covered the question of ground handling. In these the Messerschmitt did well, for apart from some harsh use required on the brakes and some lively use of the throttle in small spaces, manoeuvrability was good.

Of greater interest, however, was the comparison of the enemy type with its British counterpart under conditions of simulated combat and the procedure before this was for the two types to take off independently and to rendezvous at 6,000 feet. The meeting made, the Messerschmitt pilot would then draw away and trials would commence to discover which fighter could out-turn the other and, to eliminate all possibility of human considerations, this was repeated with the pilots changing places. In all such manoeuvres the Nazi machine proved to be at a disadvantage, having the larger turning circle. This was not so in a straight comparison of speed, for here the Messerschmitt enjoyed a small superiority, although the state of affairs was not regarded as serious. But what did prove disquieting was the finding as to the ease with which Luftwaffe pilots had been able to break off combat at will under actual fighting conditions.

It had long been reported from operational units that to

break away from an engagement it was only necessary for a Messerschmitt pilot to fling down the nose of his machine and pass straight into a screaming dive going hell-bent almost into the vertical. There was a strong clue as to what was going on when these facts were examined along with reports of what happened when RAF pilots attempted to follow, for in so doing they always complained that at the very moment that maximum power was vital their Merlins would hesitate, cough out a burst of petrol-blue smoke and then pick up again.

At this period the problem of pilots blacking out was well understood, having been encountered in the earlier Schneider Trophy Contest's later days, and something very similar was happening here in that centrifugal forces were draining away liquid at an all-important moment. The difference was that whereas in most combat manoeuvres a pilot is situated on the inside of a circle he was now on the outside and in such a situation, while the human frame could cope with the sudden change of velocity from the horizontal to the near-vertical after comparatively little complaint, the same was not true of the aircraft fuel systems.

The difference lay in the fact that the Messerschmitt enjoyed the advantages of direct fuel injection to the Daimler-Benz motor and by comparison the Merlin suffered the restrictions of a carburettor. In conditions of actual combat pilots flying Spitfires had evolved a method of overcoming this and during earlier encounters it was a usual sight to see the British fighters flung on to their backs before following an adversary down so that the direction of the negative force of gravity (G) was reversed in relation to the airframe. However, this was not regarded as good enough and in order to rectify matters a floatless carburettor was devised for the Merlin in a matter of only a few days so that the vital seconds lost in flipping a Spitfire on to its back before a dive were now saved.

Work of discovering secrets such as these continued

Hugh Dowding, the victor of the Battle of Britain, who had to fight under constant threat of compulsory retirement and was finally dismissed with scant recognition

Keith Park, who commanded No. 11 Group throughout the summer of 1940 and who had previously been Dowding's trusted assistant, kept in touch with matters in the field by means of unheralded visits, as did his own right-hand man

The badge of No. 11 Group incorporates a representation of Big Ben, indicating that London's Westminster formed part of the heart of the defence area

Pilots of No. 19 Squadron in the summer of 1940. This photograph emphasizes the fact that the majority of the pilots were NCOs. The lack of ties was a precaution by some against shrinkage and strangulation, which might result from being brought down in the sea

5.25 p.m. on 20th May in Victoria Embankment Gardens, showing just how close total war had come to the civilian world in No. 11 Group in 1940. Burns's statue is to the left of the RAF trailer in the middle distance and the tip of Cleopatra's Needle shows above the balloon

The same spot on 7th July 1981. Fewer landmarks are to be seen as the trees are upwards of forty years more mature

Frequently all those on the earth knew of a battle at height was the pattern of vapour trails in the sky. Here such a tracery is seen over the guns of a vessel in a Channel convoy in June, this being the southern boundary of 11 Group's area

July's middle days saw great aerial activity over the English Channel, where several convoys were attacked. Here bombs from a dive-bomber fall aft of a destroyer

Dover Harbour was the target for about fifty raiders on 19th July, the salvoes of bombs throwing up spectacular fountains of water as seen here

A Spitfire of No. 65 Squadron at Hornchurch is refuelled on Monday 5th August. Code letters were FZ-O while the serial number N3165 appeared in six-inch numerals, slightly smaller than standard, under the tail-plane. Chalked on the vertical airscrew blade are the words "NOT TURN"

Top: At 7.10 a.m. on 13th August, Oberleutnant Paul Temme, Gruppe Adjutant of I/JG2, had to force-land his Messerschmitt 109E-1 close to Shoreham Airport. The rails in the background mark the adjacent railway track

Above: The pall of smoke from Tangmere's blazing hangars after the dive-bombers' attack on 16th August

Below: With an Army Second Lieutenant in the foreground, a Messerschmitt 109 lies on Surrey farmland. This is believed to be WNr6204 of 1/JG54 shot down over Dungeness at 7.15 on 28th August by Squadron Leader Denholm of No. 603 Squadron. Pilot of the enemy machine, which was marked with a prominent "4", was Feldwebel Schoettle, who was captured when the aircraft fell on Copt Hill Farm, Capel

Memorial to Sergeant Peter K. Walley at Merton Technical College,
London Road, Morden

The Junkers 88 that came down on 15th August over Hampshire
farmland, witnessed by Mr Fry. The guard is supplied by an Australian
soldier in front of the starboard wing

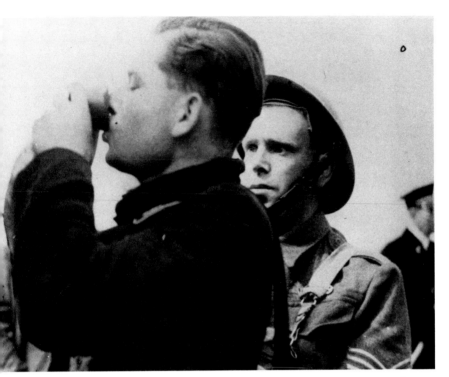

A young Leutnant, after being rescued from the sea, quenches his thirst while a British Army sergeant looks on. The date was 28th August and his unit 6/KG3

The same Luftwaffe officer is assisted by a private and lance corporal while a civil policeman brings up the rear. Retention of breeches and boots was popular with Nazi airmen at the time. The badge on the left breast of the Leutnant's uniform is his pilot's qualification, the equivalent of British "wings". His Dornier 17Z had come down off Margate throughout the lengthening days of June in the month's grace that circumstances had seemed to give England, so that questions concerning the space, comfort, noise level and view from the Messerschmitt cockpit were all answered as the time ran out. In general the Nazi design received a favourable report from the Farnborough test team, and the Daimler-Benz motor came in for special praise. The controls of this proved of attractive simplicity and the throttle with no override came in for special note.

One feature that was often commented on in the popular press at the time was that the Nazi fighter had only a side-hinged canopy and it was certainly true that this prevented an ideal view when taxi-ing as this had to be carried out with the hood closed; nevertheless in normal flight the frames gave no problems of view and as a consequence of the closed conditions of this top it was possible to maintain high speed under even poor weather conditions with the aid of the clear-view aperture.

But now the four short weeks of June 1940 were running out. It had been a month of fevered activity as the defenders of these islands worked like men and women possessed, scarcely believing their luck that a short breathing-space had been given, every day expecting that the time of tensioned calm would evaporate. While the "haloed-Wellingtons"—modified bombers with 60-foot-diameter magnetic rings, energized at low flight to deal with the new menace of magnetic mines in such vital shipping lanes as that of the Thames Estuary—did their solitary work, the final touches were put to the defence system that should have been carried out in the days of peace and to which such men as Dowding had contributed what they could and had continued to do so even up to defying Churchill and denying further defence to the French in a battle already lost. "Why doesn't he come?" asked the inhabitants of south-east England in a phrase that penetrated even to the corridors of power in Nazi Germany. In a matter of days now "he", as service personnel and civilians alike were apt to describe the enemy, would come with a vengeance the like of which English shores had never before seen, and to defend them there was drawn only the thin blue line epitomized by No. 11 Group with, Drake-like at its head, the brilliant tactician Keith Park. Even at Squadron level, all was prepared in minute detail including the frequent changes of colour scheme, blue to black and white, and back to blue once more, both with and without roundels, measures said at the time to distinguish the underparts of the Hurricanes from those captured and likely to be used again when the Nazis overran France.

CHAPTER SIX

Duel in the Sun

On Monday 1st July, the dawn broke on a fine, clear morning with, some later claimed, an almost theatrical quality. However this may be, it is certainly true that the opening of the new month brought with it a fresh and almost tangible spirit that here was the stuff of which history is made, for it was manifestly evident that for all practical purposes the British nation now stood alone as it had not done against an enemy since facing the threat from Napoleon's armies during another summer one hundred and twenty-five years before, or as she had stood poised to repel the invasion which must have followed the defeat, had this taken place, of the English ships by the Spanish Armada in the reign of the first Queen Elizabeth.

Preparations to meet the new assault were taking place all over the area defended by No. 11 Group of Fighter Command and beyond, and these varied from the reduction of

Dover's population by more than half to the secret preparations of the feed pipes which were to pump petrol on to the sea to be set alight in the midst of an invasion fleet. Indeed so secret was the work that the men who prepared the pipe-lines in Dover's Packet Yard had no idea on what they were working. To underline the gravity of the situation, if there were any who now doubted the Nazis' plans to invade these shores, that same Monday morning found hidden in the thick mist that was gathered along the north coast of France an army poised to take over the island of Jersey and later its neighbours without a shot being fired, for so serious was the situation that Britain's severely mauled Army had to be reserved for the defence of the Motherland proper.

Meanwhile there were other emergency measures being taken in every walk of life and at the meeting of that day's War Cabinet, Sir Archibald Sinclair, Secretary of State for Air in the Churchill government since May, had announced that pilots' training courses were to be shortened, the number of instructional schools increased, and the RAF was to borrow pilots from the Royal Navy to augment those trained fighter pilots already with the squadrons. With an anticipated dearth of men to fly the interceptors such as these measures indicated, at squadron level every available man was welcome and it was on this same 1st July that at Kenley in Surrey his former colleagues welcomed back to No. 615, 819018, Sergeant Peter K. Walley. He had been a founder member of the squadron and had formerly been a fitter, but before the unit had left for France he had been selected for pilot training, the only one from the ranks to have been, and had now returned to his old station, flying from which he was to die still in his twentieth year forty-nine days later.

The early days of July found No. 11 Group making the final touches to the order of battle for the fight which was now inevitable, and among the innovations was the appearance of a small number of Spitfires armed with 20-millimetre cannon, excellent weapons that at the time were of only limited use due to problems with the feed mechanism, so that they were eventually replaced by those with the conventional eight rifle-calibre machine guns. Hurricanes armed with the new cannon came slightly later in the battle, but by October even a few Heinkel 111 bombers were carrying similar guns for defence.

Meanwhile the news bulletins of early July began to take on an even more ominous sound, for by the Wednesday came intelligence that the Nazi troops in occupied Norway were being increased by, amongst others, parachute troops, and at the same time, with the shipping already gathered in the ports, there was sufficient to move two divisions. Similar troop movements were noted in the Baltic ports where some small vessels had been requisitioned and hastily converted into armed patrol ships. The same was true elsewhere, as there were also reported to be troop concentrations in Holland and two airborne divisions were certainly moved into Belgium before the first Wednesday in July. To all this was added the fact that the air wings, so recently established in the occupied countries, were being further strengthened and the Calais area was now protected by continuous Luftwaffe patrols, a fact which strongly hinted that something boding no good to Britain's immediate future was being acted out there.

The Nazi Air Force was not only active over the opposite side of the Channel, for the weather now seemed to indicate a summer such as all Englishmen dream of but seldom in their lives enjoy, and the promise of long sunny days was to provide the enemy with a chance to harass coastal targets, sometimes attacking others further inland under cover of darkness. Chief amongst the towns destined to suffer was inevitably Dover, which even in these early July days began to earn its name of "Hellfire Corner", although the residents which remained found greater cause for complaint from the restrictions on their freedom such as that which forbade their being on the sea front after the fall of darkness. Symptomatic of the strange atmosphere of expectation and the end of an older way of life was the air of mixed waiting and desolation found by servicemen and civilians alike. The steamers of the Southern Railway had gone north from the Kentish front-line town, and excepting the handful which remained for harbour work with the gallant little cutter *Pioneer* in constant use, the Cinque Ports Pilots had all moved to Gravesend.

It was these early July days which saw 11 Group's first brushes with the enemy. At this time the majority of the single machines that appeared over the coast were bent on reconnaissance, but all the signs pointed to a great assault that was soon to crystallize.

Dawn on 4th July was marked by a continuance of the promise of the previous days and it was now that the first concerted Luftwaffe attacks were delivered against this country. As far as No. 11 Group was concerned the main attack was not to be delivered until the early afternoon when a force of enemy aircraft attacked a small convoy steaming through the Dover Straits. Scrambled to meet this were the Hurricanes of No. 79 Squadron flying from Hawkinge, yet scarcely had the handful of interceptors reached the bombers than they in turn were set upon by the Messerschmitts sent to protect the larger machines and after an inconclusive encounter in which none of the enemy machines was claimed, one of the Hurricanes was seen to be screaming earthwards out of control to take its sergeant-pilot to his death near St Margaret's Bay, Dover.

The evening of the same day brought a new succession of Hostile plots to the Operations Room tables of the Group and a skirmish in the light of the sinking sun took place, as the hands of the clock crept towards 7 p.m., between Messerschmitt 109s and No. 32 Squadron's Hurricanes over Dungeness. In the first few moments of the encounter, the Nazis scored and two of the Hurricanes went down, both without hurt to the pilots, one managing to make a forced landing on the airfield at Hawkinge. Of the Messerschmitts, one was accounted for when it plunged into the sea and was lost, and another from JG27 is claimed to have been damaged after this brief encounter when making an emergency landing in France.

No. 11 Group's Battle of Britain had begun therefore with no great encounter of giants and at the time there was no indication of the manner in which it would unfold. Keith Park was obviously husbanding his forces at this period since it was obvious to all that the storm would break with considerably greater force in the near future if an invasion was to be attempted and this could only be broken by the defenders in the air.

The following Friday saw a break in the promised fine weather and the skies took on an almost wintry look as the grey ten-tenths cloud covered the greater part of south-east England. No doubt Hugh Dowding found this in entire accord with the uncertainty of his personal life up to that time, but that same morning he received a request to postpone his retirement from the service which had been scheduled for nine days hence. It was evident that although the future of the country was in deadly peril, the processes of a correctly ordered administration must go on without interruption.

This deterioration in the weather had its effect on the enemy too, yet as the RDF plots showed, "he" was by no means inactive although a number of sorties were recalled to base. One interception which was made took place before 7 o'clock in the morning when a Heinkel 111 was reported in the vicinity of Dover. This proved to be a machine of KG1's No. 8 Staffel and it quickly became a target for no less than nine Spitfires from No. 65 Squadron based at Hornchurch. The bomber was quite swiftly despatched by three of the pilots, one of whom, Flying Officer G. Proudman, could he have but known, having only two days more of life left to him, thus representing the expectation of survival at the time which fighter pilots had. The bomber was driven down off Dover's Lydden Spout and two of the crew managed to swim ashore where they were taken prisoner. Later in the day the same district was to receive six bombs near to the breakwater, where a sapper was wounded, the single raider in the meanwhile escaping unharmed.

The following day, 6th July, saw an improvement in the weather in the north although in No. 11 Group's area it remained much as it had been. Even so there was some enemy air activity and a blip on the RDF screens a little after 5 a.m. in the morning turned out to be a single raider flying at a great height where the sounds of an exchange of gunfire seemed to indicate an interception. In fact this attack was to be of minor historic note since the ten bombs which were dropped were to be the first actually to explode on Dover soil, the sound of the first being noted at exactly twenty minutes past five in the morning. For the most part the bombs fell in open country, the stick crossing Coombe Farm to a point near to Buckland Rectory via Bunker's Hill.

By now it was evident that something momentous was about to take place in the very near future and the news-papers read in home, pub, club and mess took on an air of hopeful optimism with the telling of odd tales concerning the limited fighting which had up to that time taken place. One incident which was well illustrated at the time showed the remains of a Dornier 17Z which had careered through a hop garden to break up finally among the vines. In fact the incident had taken place three days before but the filtering through of news was often slow at the time due to the demands of an over-worked censor. With the pictures had come a curious story, for it seems that a farmer was nearby and driving his tractor, the engine note of which drowned all other sounds. Great was his surprise therefore when he was suddenly confronted in one of his own fields by a figure in Nazi uniform stiffly saluting him. His astonishment was increased when, having turned off the motor, he was able to hear the newcomer tell him in English without a trace of an accent that he had managed to scramble out of the wrecked Dornier and that he now wished to surrender. "Well," said the farmer, recovering his composure, "I suppose you'd better come over to my house", and the Nazi was conducted away to be given a cup of tea while waiting for a police escort to arrive. As the battle advanced these chance encounters with the enemy became less cordial and there is on record another story within No. 11 Group of the pilot of a Messerschmitt, wounded and in pain, having escaped by parachute, who, on knocking at the door of a suburban house explained in his first words to the man who answered that he was a fighter pilot, not from a bomber. This was a wise precaution for at much the same time one of the crewmen who escaped from the aircraft that crashed in the forecourt of Victoria Station in London was so severely beaten by civilians before the police could rescue him that, coupled with his wounded condition, he was subsequently to die from the ill-treatment received.

Sunday, 7th July, was another day of indifferent weather, yet ironically it had been chosen by Hitler and announced four days before as the date on which the Victory Parade was to take place in Paris following a ceremonial entry into the city. In fact this was postponed and at the same time an increase in the activities of the Luftwaffe over the British Isles was noted.

First indications of the increase over the area defended by No. 11 Group had taken place during the hours of darkness when some bombs had been dropped in Surrey and Hampshire despite a very heavy barrage of anti-aircraft fire, which although of value as a civilian morale-booster, achieved exactly nothing.

The day's events began quietly enough, much in the manner of those which had marked the preceding days leading to little more than skirmishes, with only reconnaissance flights being reported on the flickering cathode-ray tubes in the Operations Rooms. These seemed to indicate a persistent interest in a convoy proceeding eastwards past the Isle of Wight and two of the shadowing Dorniers were sent down before 10.30 a.m. one falling into the sea near to the Needles, while a third was destroyed after noon across the Channel from Bognor Regis. Even so, these and the unusual activity of groups of free-hunting interceptors had the effect of keeping the sector stations in the vicinity on their toes, but it was not until the convoy had made its slow progress into the Dover Strait by 9.30 p.m. that the real intentions of the enemy became clear. It was now that the first real air battle was fought over Dover and it was such a novelty that people stood in the streets to watch what eye-witnesses recall as more than fifty aircraft locked in battle. Occasionally one of the machines would detach itself and plummet earthwards and the sight of one brought a particularly hearty cheer from some, who were ignorant that it was one of the defending Spitfires that they were watching fall to its demise in Hougham Woods where it burst into flames. These seem to have been the final moments in the life of Flying Officer G. Proudman, the victor of the encounter a few days previously.

Meanwhile five bombs exploded in the harbour area indicating that the enemy had something of a free hand, for the real target was obviously the ships and not land targets. The reason for this was that although the RDF plots had been correctly interpreted in time, the Spitfires scrambled from Hornchurch and Kenley had been sent off too late and the consequence was that the majority of the Dorniers had dropped their loads and were setting course for home before the Spitfires arrived with those from Kenley in the lead. The result was that although some victories had been scored they were somewhat empty ones since the convoy had not been properly protected.

It was now clear what was the exact form of the war which 11 Group of Fighter Command had to be prepared to fight, for the position looked dangerously like one where fighters would be engaged for long periods of time with little result and the arm slowly worn away in consequence.

Monday brought a confirmation of this grave situation for another convoy was obviously being shadowed at a time when there were several to choose from, that picked out having probably been selected for its size and seeming importance since it had left the mouth of the Thames under cover of darkness. The pattern began to fall into place when the RDF stations reported what appeared to be a build-up of aircraft over the sea off Calais so that extra cover was immediately ordered for the ships. A part of this force achieved nothing more than the interception of a Heinkel 111 which alerted the Dover anti-aircraft batteries on the first of two occasions that morning.

However, it was not until about 2 a.m. that the first major interception of a bombing force took place, although its intentions were obscure so that the civilian warning was sounded in all the coastal towns likely to be attacked. The running battle which followed was at first an encounter between Dorniers and Spitfires alone but it was not long before the Hurricanes of No. 79 Squadron were sent off. The result was something of a disaster, for the system of free-hunting single-seaters used by the enemy on previous occasions now began to pay increased dividends. The Messerschmitts pounced on the unsuspecting pilots of the Hawker machines and two went down immediately, one, erroneously reported as a Spitfire at the time, taking Flying Officer Mitchell to a horrible death in the flaming wreckage of his machine, which continued to burn for over an hour at Green Lane, Temple Ewell, a few miles beyond the centre of Dover.

It was soon after this that the long-awaited main attack on the convoy was judged not to be coming, since the action shortly afterwards faded out, perhaps following the discovery that the ships below carried no cargo.

Weather still provided the chief problem for defenders and attackers alike on the next day, 9th July, which was of historical interest in that it was the date on which the élite Messerschmitt 110s were first used. They were soon being provided with an escort to remedy their inability to defend themselves alone, but the Luftwaffe was still committed to the policy of destroying the Royal Air Force by small degrees of wasteful action.

As a preliminary to this the reconnaissance branch of the Luftwaffe was active once more just before mid-morning since if convoys were to be the main targets, plans to attack them had to be formulated at short notice, a policy which had its beginnings in the measures of the earlier conflict. However, the raids of this particular day, although locally intense with huge numbers of raiders being sent off, making it the most strenuous day to date, did not over all result in a victory for either side. The real value of 9th July lay in the fact that Keith Park had at last a chance to gain practical experience in the art of breaking up large numbers of hostile machines with a relatively small fighter force.

June had been significant as the month when Erprobungsgruppe 210 had been activated. This was a specialist unit operating with Luftflotte 2 theoretically to evaluate the Messerschmitt 110 and 109 fighter-bombers with which it had been equipped first at Lille, the personnel, equipment and aircraft having in the main been drawn from ZG1. A period of dive-bomber training had been carried out in Denmark a little later and the official formation of the unit had then taken place at Koln-Ostheim before transfer to Denaîn in northern France on 10th July, there to begin its operational career three days later with shipping attacks that were to be its speciality for the time being.

Yet this second Wednesday in July was certainly the day when the pace of air operations was seen to quicken and with this acceleration came the type of fighting and casualties which were to mark the remainder of the summer. Not all the losses in battle were to be brought about by gunfire, as a glance at the combat reports shows today, and one of the earliest collisions resulting in the death of a British pilot is recorded for this day.

Flying Officer T. P. K. Higgs had taken off with others of No. 111 Squadron from Croydon, the London Airport of the pre-war years, to intercept an attack by Dornier 17Z

bombers on another convoy off Folkestone. The Hurricanes
had encountered a huge formation of attackers and had
passed this in order to commence stern attacks. After some
exchange of fire with the aircraft of 3/KG2 which accounted
for one of the enemy, Higgs was seen to collide with
another of the Dorniers, although there were those who
believed that he had deliberately rammed the bomber. This
seems doubtful but what is certain is that a moment later the
wing of the fighter was seen to fall away while the greater
part of the Hurricane with the pilot still aboard dropped
away like a stone. From this, Higgs was seen to escape by
parachute, only to plummet into the ocean. "A rescue
launch was despatched immediately," records the
Squadron diary, but the crew failed to discover any sign of
the fate of either the British pilot or those aboard the Dornier
which had likewise dropped into the Channel.

Meanwhile the spirit of "business as usual", a strong
contribution to victory in its own way, moved the Civil
Service to ensure that Hugh Dowding's deferred rétirement
date was notified in writing while, probably more to the
immediate point, the War Cabinet met to discuss the draft
of the booklet on anti-invasion measures which was in a
short while, to be distributed to every household in the
nation.

On the opposite side of the English Channel the enemy
air striking units were divided into twin Luftflotten,
Number 2 with its headquarters in Brussels and Number 3
which was commanded from Paris. Number 3 was the
responsibility of Generalfeldmarschall Sperrle, but perhaps
of greater interest is the name associated with Fliegerkorps
VIII, operating from the Le Havre peninsula, General
Wolfram von Richthofen, a relative of the "Red Baron" of
twenty-two years before. The surname was now coupled
with Junkers 87 dive-bombers, and it was a raid by these
which set out to attack a convoy on 11th July, the opposition
being provided by 501 Squadron's Hurricanes and the
Spitfires of 609 Squadron. In the event the interception was

a disaster, for the Hurricanes were set upon by the Messerschmitt 109s providing escort and the Spitfires found themselves fighting at odds of six to one, so that the most they could hope for was to harass the enemy and in this at least they were successful, although one of the Naval vessels was sent to the bottom.

The same day also saw an attack of a different type, for Heinkel 111s of 1 and 2/KG55 were directed against Portsmouth on the periphery of No. 11 Group's area. Hurricanes were quickly scrambled to intercept and a running fight ensued up the Solent, although the defenders were unable to prevent the bombers from dropping their loads on Portsmouth with its dockyard and important works. Several of the raiders paid the ultimate price for their bravery, and one of the machines passed into local history. This was the Heinkel which fell at about 6.15 p.m. and was the first enemy aircraft to be brought down in West Sussex, crashing a short way off the shore at East Beach, Selsey, killing Unteroffizier Mueller and Oberfeldwebel Schlueter in the process, although the remainder of the crew survived to be taken captive.

As the pace of battle increased the defenders as well as attackers fell in increasing numbers, although on occasion it could be "friendly" forces that brought down a machine. Such a case was that of one of the Royal Navy pilots now operating to augment the strength of Fighter Command. There were two such officers, Sub-Lieutenants Dawson Paul and Sykes flying from the Sector Station at Kenley where No. 64 Squadron was based.

Both were on patrol on Saturday 13th July in a sky which had now taken a turn to the better conditions expected of a summer's day and at 15,000 feet the blue expanse provided a contrasting backdrop to the chalk of the Dover cliffs below. The formation of nine Spitfires had been vectored to intercept another approaching enemy formation, when from below without warning the trigger-happy gunners of an anti-aircraft emplacement suddenly opened up with a deadly accurate fire. For Sykes the first intimation of events took the form of a sudden explosion ahead of him, throwing his machine almost over on to its back as the cockpit filled with the stench of explosive. As he righted the machine the fact flashed through his mind that his second sortie was about to end in an ignominious belly landing, for in the same moment he realized that the Spitfire was badly hit, with the engine failing and the hydraulics shot away.

It seemed a long way to Kenley's advanced landing ground at Hawkinge and with the fire-tender making a flash of colour in the distance, John Sykes slid his machine to a grinding, jolting halt as the straps of his harness bit into his shoulders with the violence of the deceleration. Then all seemed quiet for a moment before the pilot scrambled out in case the seemingly inevitable fire broke out. He stood for a moment and glanced at the sky where the whirling contrails marked the place where his RAF colleagues were now locked in combat with the enemy. Suddenly he stared hard in disbelief, for there straight ahead of him was another winged Spitfire seeking the sanctuary of Hawkinge. This time it was a Sergeant Binham's machine that had fallen victim to the gunners' faulty identification.

Meanwhile there was little doubt that the aerial activity was the run-up to the invasion of the British Isles and on the same day that Sykes had suffered his dramatic landing, Hitler had written to Mussolini declining the offer made a little earlier of Italian troops to assist in the coming assault on the beleagured fortress-island.

Meanwhile, there had settled in at Kenley a prolific diary-keeper, "Sammy" Samson, an engine fitter with No. 615 Squadron, and for the following day, 14th July, he recalls a set of events that typified No. 11 Group's summer.

The Squadron had been engaged with enemy formations over the Channel in the afternoon following a morning of little activity. Dive-bombers were much in evidence, for the few machines that had been encountered before lunch were evidently bent on reconnaissance to find likely convoys as targets. The Junkers 87s had been about forty in number with an escort of Messerschmitt 109s and to the guns of one of these, Samson recalls, Pilot Officer M. R. Mudie had fallen victim. The incident had happened at exactly 3.30 p.m. when a burst from a machine of II/JG51 had sent KW G, L1584 plummeting towards the sea with Mudie, gravely wounded, struggling to get out. In this he succeeded and parachuted into the Channel from which he was rescued by the Royal Navy, but so serious were his injuries that the young 24-year-old officer died in Dover Hospital the following day.

This was the action of which BBC commentator Charles Gardner made the now-famous "running-commentary" record that was broadcast less than three hours later on the 6 p.m. news bulletin, but the observer on the coast could see only a part of the action and could take no account of the machines that limped home from the flight, such as that flown by Pilot Officer Eyres, who managed to bring back his Hurricane although badly shot up.

The convoy that had been the target was code-named "Bread" and the damage inflicted was at the time claimed to have been slight, a loss of seven aircraft to the Nazis, one of these being seen to crash spectacularly into the sea within sight of watchers on the cliffs, this probably being the Ju 87 brought down by two pilots (Collard and Hugo) of the Kenley Squadron. Three ships, one of them a Norwegian vessel, were hit by bombs, including HMS *Vanessa* which was later towed into Dover Harbour by the tug *Lady Duncannon*, which soon after put to sea again to bring in the SS *Balder* of Bergen. She had suffered damage to her stern where the anti-aircraft gun had been put out of action, and the chief officer and three members of the crew had been killed by bomb splinters. Other vessels damaged included the *Gronland* and the *Island Queen*, of which two crew-members had perished.

This then was the pattern of the earliest days of No. 11 Group's Battle of Britain, with a seeming attempt to wear down the defenders in the manner of the successful Nazi campaign that had made them the masters of Europe. To this the weather had only occasionally been of some help, for although the memory of 1940 today is of unbroken sunny days, at this particular time it was indifferent, improving and assisting the enemy seeking land targets only later, although the cloud over the Channel in mid-month had been remarked on as ideal for attacks on shipping. This fact was ignored on the following day when the low cloud merited an entry in Samson's diary: "Very bad weather, no flying today but Squadron at readiness."

CHAPTER SEVEN

Time for a Beer-Up

Despite the build-up of activity that had taken place up to now, there followed a pause in the air fighting about mid-month and when the raiders resumed their visits it was still to pound mainly targets in the Channel. Hitler marked the period with the now well-known Directive No. 16, the seven copies issued containing the threat that a landing in England was to be prepared for, and if necessary carried out. The operation was to be completed by mid-August, although this was later changed to name 15th September as the final date owing to the deterioration in the weather which was likely to follow.

Although there were occasional visitations by enemy bombers by night, Sector B marked the quiet time in its own peculiar way, which was a means of using up the collection accumulated by 615 Squadron's fines. These were demanded for a wide range of "crimes", ranging from one penny for dirty buttons to one of ten shillings (50p) for shooting down an RAF aircraft, although no one is sure if this one was actually ever paid! Intermediate felonies might cost sixpence (2½p), the fine exacted for failing to salute a "B" Flight officer; although those of "A" Flight were rated at only half this figure. During this July the Valley Hotel at Caterham in Surrey rang with merriment as the fine kitty was opened over the bar.

It was during this time that a peculiar incident took place. The first part of the tale is that which is well known, namely the case of floatplanes being shot down despite their Red Cross markings when it was alleged in England that their missions were not devoted entirely to acts of mercy. Less commonly remembered is the fact that contemporary notes tell of one such machine deliberately wading in to a complete British fighter squadron while on patrol so that, as one serviceman at the time pointed out, the Nazi pilot in theory was committing suicide.

At this time there also came to the fore a part of the Army's activities in No. 11 Group. Comparatively unknown amongst this was the work performed by the motor coach companies, their transport in the main being civilian buses painted khaki. Duties consisted of those men from the 7th Pioneer Battalion of the York and Lancaster Regiment touring coastal areas of special vulnerability to dig and mine anti-tank ditches in addition to erecting wire barricades. When not at work the men were confined to camp and were allowed out only for a single day per week to take a bath, albeit equipped with full kit, rifle and twenty rounds of ammunition for the journey.

In common with so many armed units of the time, these companies suffered a serious shortage of equipment and it is on record that one detachment had only a single anti-tank rifle and a Bren gun for training purposes. Ironically, some of the NCOs had seen masses of equipment destroyed and abandoned during the retreat from northern France when they had been serving with the Cameronians, the King's

Own Scottish Borderers or the Highland Light Infantry. These regiments had all seen hard fighting in the spring and early summer of that same year and now formed the hard core of the companies which included in their duties the removal of human remains, equipment and manuals from crashed enemy aircraft, the latter items being carefully set aside for examination by the Intelligence service.

Another army contribution to the survival of the RAF Groups was that supplied by the Royal Engineers, who were employed on the repair of damaged airfields. At that time there existed no organization within the RAF for this type of work, so a number of general construction companies were briefed for the work, there being 134 airfields with maintenance parties available by the end of June. An alternative was to use civilian labour and this was done in some parts despite the problems of ensuring that the work for which they were assigned was in fact carried out, for these labour forces showed a marked tendency to go to cover when the raid warning was given and then refuse to emerge. Not being subject to military discipline there was little that could be done about this except resort to promise of reward or blandishment. Wing Commander Victor Beamish, then the station commander at North Weald, is on record as having tried threats but all were equally ineffective. Finally there was nothing for it at these stations but to put parties of airmen on the job, thus making probably the first step in the formation of the uniformed Airfield Construction Units. In the meantime huge piles of rubbish were made available at aerodromes to be at hand for filling bomb craters.

The drizzle which had marked the middle days of July over most of the country, including that covered by No. 11 Group, ensured that the temporary respite from battle continued for a short while longer and the chief type of Luftwaffe activity was still a series of attacks on Channel convoys with the object of luring 11 Group's fighter force into the air to be slowly worn away, a tactic to which the low cloud of the prevailing weather particularly lent itself. From the south coast it was possible to deduce that there was considerable if localized aerial activity out at sea although this was nearly always accompanied by the civilian warning being sounded, often with nothing resulting.

The reverse was true, however, of Friday, 19th July, the day after the postponed Nazi victory parade had taken place through Paris, the first time that German troops had marched through that city since 1871, sixty-nine years before. The day opened without much activity, although a Dornier 17P slipped unnoticed through the defences and remained undetected until it was within twelve or so miles of London, over Croydon in Surrey, from whence it was chased out to sea and finally shot down off Brighton.

The main activity of the day was marked during the afternoon by a very determined attack on Dover Harbour by Junkers 87s which the British RDF had "seen" gathering over the Pas de Calais about an hour before. Eye-witnesses recall the attack as one of the most spectacular up to that time with the exploding bombs flinging up great fountains of water to the accompaniment of an intense anti-aircraft barrage. This was one of the first occasions when the new Parachute and Cable (PAC) device was tried out, a system whereby a small parachute fired in the path of oncoming bombers opened to drift slowly down with a length of lethal cable suspended underneath. One of these, undetonated, caused some consternation when it lodged over the entrance to the railway tunnel behind Dover's Oil Mills until it was removed by the Royal Navy.

It was through a curtain of fire that the defending fighters had to fly to get to grips with the enemy which were well defended themselves by an escort of Messerschmitt 109s that had their fuel supplies less stretched over a target such as this compared with attacks on a target further inland.

Chief among the ships destroyed in the harbour was the *War Sepoy*, an Admiralty tanker of 11,500 tons which had her back broken by a bomb that scored a near miss. Later this vessel was towed to the western entrance of the harbour and there sunk as a block ship to make further defence against the invaders whose coming was regarded as certain.

Claims at the time that of the 120 raiders eleven were brought down made no mention of the British losses for this day, extending as they did to the virtual annihilation of No. 141 Squadron flying two-seat Defiant fighters from dispersal at Hawkinge. It was one of these machines that crashed at Elms Vale, Dover, blowing up in the roadway there and killing the pilot, Flight Lieutenant Donald, who is reported to have remained aboard too long in order to permit his gunner to escape by parachute, although in the event the sacrifice would seem to have been in vain for no trace of the second crew-member was ever discovered.

This July Friday was also eventful inland in a different way, for it was the day chosen by King George VI for one of his periodic visits to RAF stations, in this case Northolt. These tours were of great value in the wartime years, not only to military establishments but to places laid waste by bombing where the presence of various members of the royal family did far more to keep up public morale than numerous broadcast exhortations by politicians. On this occasion observers in the area, who had been surprised and puzzled five days earlier by the appearance of a strange, new twin-motor fighter which was the then highly secret Westland Whirlwind, were treated on the occasion of the royal visit to the sight of a veritable galaxy of different service machines, gathered to perform a fly-past. Bristol Beauforts, Blenheims, Whitley bombers, Hudsons, Hampdens, Hurricanes, Spitfires and Wellingtons were all to be seen. On a graver note it was the same day which saw the announcement that the twenty-mile-deep Defence Area, where movement was restricted, had now been further extended by additions in Dorset.

The subject of the royal visits also recalls an amusing tale of one such to another fighter station in No. 11 Group. On this occasion two members of a ground crew were mentally congratulating themselves on not being guard of honour material for they preferred to do something more practical. Thus it was that the pair found themselves changing the radiator and fairing on a Hawker Hurricane that had been damaged.

The two were by now liberally soaked with glycol and one had a badly cut finger. They were toiling well away from the area of the station headquarters where the royal visitor was likely to be. However, King George was not one to accept the sight of only what his officers deemed it suitable for him to see and the party with the King had wandered away to inspect the maintenance area. At that particular moment, one of the men was crouched uncomfortably under the fighter and, facing aft while his colleague helped, was attempting to align the fastened holes of the new fairing with the attachment anchor nuts. With this both were having some difficulty and one was relieving his feelings with a colourful flow of language. This terminated in mid-sentence when he was nudged by the other, who was turning perceptibly pale, for there looking down at them was the King himself! "This man appears to be having a spot of bother," observed His Majesty to his companion who, from all that was to be seen of him by the two on the ground, might well have been an Air Marshal at least. Then with a smile at the upturned and blood-stained face of the nearer man, the King turned away with a distinct chuckle at the graphic description of recalcitrant fastenings which had been overheard!

Convoys continued to provide the main targets for the Luftwaffe's attention, as if to underline the threat of imminent invasion. Certainly this was uppermost in the minds of the Government, which was finally debating the creation of a Special Operations Executive. This was to be presided over by the Minister of Economic Warfare, his deputy being in charge of co-ordinating subversive and sabotage measures. But two days before this was announced No. 11

Group of Fighter Command had achieved its first real victory over the enemy. The occasion of this had been when yet another convoy had entered the protection of B and C Sectors and it was here that at about 6 p.m. the ships were singled out for the attention of Junkers 87s, the Stukas that had swept across Europe and against which there seemed to be no defence. Now, with an escort of Messerschmitts the Nazi pilots found themselves flying into the descending sun and it is probably due to this that they failed to see the large force of Hurricanes and Spitfires that Keith Park had scrambled to safeguard the ships. The resultant fight took upwards of half an hour to reach a conclusion and at the end of it a myth had been destroyed for, at a cost of three fighters lost or damaged, the dive-bombers were routed and it was finally proven that against organized defence, and if possible the advantage of altitude, the Stuka was no more invincible than any other attacker.

It seems probable that the enemy was not immediately aware of this, for the next significant raid on the following Wednesday was once more directed against vessels at Dover which had previously been bombed twice on the victorious Saturday, the first attack sinking the 1,360-ton destroyer HMS *Brazen*, while the twenty machines mounting the assault later apparently singled out the Admiralty Pier for destruction.

On 24th July a fleet of mine-sweepers outside the harbour at Dover was attacked, but it was the following day, a Thursday, that saw the longest sustained air and sea action which had up to that time taken place within 11 Group, for the civilian alert lasted for a total of five hours on this occasion. The first raid to be reported was by about sixty enemy machines operating in concert with E-boats detailed to deal with British destroyers which were also dive-bombed. This assault took place off Lydden Spout, where a convoy of some twenty merchant vessels was suddenly set upon, four of the ships being sunk and a fifth had to be beached at Shakespeare Cliff. The Naval vessels included

HMS *Boreas* and *Brilliant* and these both sustained damage: little wonder in view of the fact that each was seen to vanish repeatedly behind veritable walls of water thrown up by the exploding bombs.

A second phase of the attack on the convoy took place off Folkestone although by now the enemy was being engaged by Spitfires of 54 Squadron, of which there were only nine, and a further eight from No. 64 Squadron, and it was at about this point that watchers on the cliffs saw smoke-screens being laid to make a dark background against which the bright flashes of the gunfire stood out boldly.

The third engagement found the convoy now in the vicinity of Shoreham with the final total of ships un-damaged and able to reach port now only three, so that an effort had to be made to assist the number of stranded vessels which, after the cessation of the main raid, could easily have been picked off by further E-boats like sitting ducks.

Among those merchantmen that finally limped home were the M.V. *Summity* which, with a badly holed hull and steering gear useless, had to be run aground for her master and several crew-members who were wounded to be taken off. Admiralty figures subsequently issued stated that five vessels, representing a total tonnage of 5,014, had been sunk and a further five, of 5,153 tons, damaged. Other merchant vessels finally to reach port were the *Gronland*, later to be sunk in another raid on Dover's outer harbour when carrying a cargo of coal; *Newminster,* soon repaired by the Southern Railway Packet Yard; *Hodder* and *Tamworth*. The destroyers also required assistance: HMS *Boreas* was stopped off Sandgate, and *Brilliant* was taken in two by Dover tugs, among which the *Lady Brassey* had to approach through a veritable rain of bombs to pass a line across the former destroyer. Between these two a total of sixteen casualties was reported, although to this must be added the officer and four ratings who later died of their wounds. The injured comprised two officers and twenty-three ratings.

Before dusk descended No. 610 Squadron had been thrown into the fray but it was past 8 p.m. before the sky over the Dover Strait was empty of aircraft.

Thursday, 25th July, may therefore be counted as the day which finally set the pattern of future events; the War Cabinet certainly saw it as such, for whereas the earlier days had seen what now appeared to be no more than exploratory actions, on this day there was a determined assault, well pressed home. A problem encountered by 11 Group on this occasion was that the fighters scrambled from such forward bases as Hawkinge had to climb in full view of the Nazi formations, so that Dowding was later to report: "You never had time to gain height before you were attacked." Confident that he had the backing of Park, who was a resourceful tactician and fighter pilot at heart, Hugh Dowding seized the opportunity the following day to attend the meeting of the Defence Committee, where the remark that convoys could hardly be expected to go on sustaining casualties like those of the previous day, drew from Sir Dudley Pound, his Naval colleague, the news that the better-armed Hunt-class destroyers being introduced into service might be expected to draw the enemy's attention in future. He added that times had changed and the future threw an increased burden on the task awaiting the Army; it certainly seemed to be the case and as if in confirmation of this, reliable sources made it clear three days later that the first movement of Nazi troops to stations facing 11 Group's southern coast had taken place.

Nevertheless, none of these rather ineffectual arguments managed to divert Dowding from the reason for his journey from Bentley Priory. Pointing out that at times "there were over one hundred aircraft over the Channel", he went on to make it clear that in much of the action fighter was engaging fighter leaving the bombers to have a comparatively free hand. Most of the merchant vessels involved, he went on, were in fact small ships carrying in the main coal, and the suspension of their activities would not amount to "a national calamity''. With this the Admiralty was forced reluctantly to agree, for by doing so it had to admit that, however temporarily, the control of the Channel had been taken from England by air power. The final decision was an example of the British flair for compromise: no more merchant sailings would take place through the narrow seas until new measures had been arrived at to ensure their safety during darkness and an improved system of escort for the daylight hours devised.

The problem that occupied Hugh Dowding's mind on the fateful Thursday which had seen such a blow to British pride over an essentially English stretch of water, is well illustrated by the experience of a pilot flying with No. 64 Squadron on 25th July, Flight Lieutenant L. F. Henstock. He was well experienced, having first flown from Kenley at the end of May although he had qualified as a pilot in 1936. At the time of the fierce convoy attack the squadron had moved to Hawkinge. Now at between six and ten thousand feet the meeting took place with a large formation of Junkers 87s protected by fighter escort over which Henstock's group had no advantage of height. Accepting this, the 64 Squadron outfit had shouted their ''Tally-ho's'' and flung themselves into the stack of Nazis, Henstock making straight for a Stuka that seemed likely meat. He fired a few bursts but was prevented from pressing home the attack due to a Messerschmitt getting on the Spitfire's tail, although small trails of smoke were seen to be coming from the Stuka. In company with another Spitfire from 64 Squadron, Henstock then saw a Messerschmitt flash across his sights and under the combined attack the fighter, probably from JG26, went down in a sheet of flame.

After a return to Hawkinge to rearm and refuel, the Flight Lieutenant was in the air again with one other Spitfire and it was not long before the controller vectored them into a situation similar to that which they had left, namely more Messerschmitts escorting further Stukas. Soon the two Spitfires were in the thick of a new mêlée and hardly had the Flight Lieutenant given another Me 109 a long burst that sent it down leaving a long streak of black smoke across the sky than he became aware of the Merlin seemingly about to shake itself from its mountings. Leaving his single colleague to fight alone, he left the battle and carefully took the Spitfire to the nearest point where it could be set down with safety, which proved to be Lympne. Meanwhile the odds against his colleague had proved too great and he had been shot down and taken prisoner, and Henstock's return to Kenley was in a Magister two-seat trainer pressed into service as a hack.

The manner in which men on either side faced being shot down was naturally different according to circumstances and individual temperament, but it was seldom as portrayed by the entertainment world; no tell-tale flash, no curl of smoke from the engine. All too often the pilot never saw the machine that gave him the *coup de grâce*: frequently the victor might begin a dive from a superior altitude, give a well-aimed burst to the victim, perhaps shooting off the tail or crippling the controls, and then carry straight on down. In circumstances such as these the first indication that a vanquished pilot received was that his machine was probably totally uncontrollable as a drop developed of the falling-leaf kind. A pilot to whom this happened recalls his reactions thus:

I had only one feeling—to get out as the heat in the cockpit was unbearable. Strangely enough my mind was quite clear as to what I must do. I unfastened my straps, crouched in the seat and gave the stick a sharp kick with my foot. This catapulted me into the air. The feeling of falling through space was extraordinary, giving a sensation of absolute freedom: quite logically I thought about pulling the rip-cord, but delayed doing so as I had no wish to pass out from lack of oxygen. When I eventually did tug on the ring I remember staring at the end in my hand and thinking of the unknown WAAF who had packed the chute and praying she had done a good job so that there I was, now floating down without a care in the world. Nearer the earth the ground came up very fast and suddenly there were Frenchmen arriving and doing their best to stop the bleeding in my leg.

July 27th was the first full day when the temporary stoppage of the Channel convoys could be seen to have taken some of the intended effect, for as was anticipated the Luftwaffe turned its attention to the Royal Navy and at the end of the day two destroyers had been damaged and a third sunk, so on the following day the remaining destroyers were withdrawn to Portsmouth.

Despite the gravity of the situation, there was no meeting of the War Cabinet until the Monday following and when it did take place the venue was the War Room deep underground at Storey's Gate instead of the stuffy Cabinet Room where the meetings normally took place. At the same time in Germany another meeting was taking place and it was at this one that a surprising suggestion was made by the Naval Staff in the light of the prevailing position. This was quite simply that there should be no attempted invasion of the British Isles until the following year.

Two days later there was something of a clarification of the position when Admiral Raeder submitted that there was a danger of the weather deteriorating and so he submitted that the invasion be postponed until the following May. This proposal was rejected and 15th September was decided as the provisional target date. The final decision regarding this was to be taken after a further week of attacks against harbours and military installations coupled with tactics designed to weaken further the RAF. Meanwhile Winston Churchill summed up the situation exactly to the House of Commons in secret session when he announced that a crisis was imminent.

Weather conditions were considerably improved for the final days of July although there was some haze that severely restricted visibility. Yet despite this every advantage was taken of the improved conditions although raids were on a small scale, often involving single aircraft, one such incident at the Kenley sector station recalled by Mr Keith Belcher, then a rigger, being typical.

No. 615 Squadron's "B" Flight was on what was known

as ten-minute readiness, a situation that called for a fitter to be seated in the Hurricane's cockpit with a rigger standing by the starter trolley. Nearby was the removable side panel giving access to the oxygen bottle and at hand too was the large screwdriver with which to replace it. When the alarm sounded the drill was for the fitter to start the engines while the pilots sprinted from the dispersal hut and meanwhile the rigger was expected to pull the trolley-accumulator clear, turn on the oxygen bottle and fit the side panel in place. On this occasion the situation was slightly different, as Pilot Officer K. T. Lofts was already in the cockpit with his RT plugged in, so that he did not hear the sinister drone of an aeroplane which seemed to have the measured beat that many associated with the enemy. Not so Mr Belcher, who looked up into the single patch of blue the sky could muster that day, only to find himself staring at what was unmistakably a lone Dornier 17 that had slipped through the defences. Ignoring the flight sergeant who was strolling by, Keith immediately ducked under the wing and shook the aileron to attract the pilot's attention, yelling at the same time to draw attention to the machine overhead.

As he doubled back to the trolley he came under the scornful gaze of the sergeant, whose turn it was to yell now. "It's people like you that cause panic," he bawled, "that's a bloody Anson, now shut up!," and so saying he strode off in the direction of his hut.

There was a moment of silence after this outburst, which was broken by a call from the cockpit, "Start-up", bellowed the pilot. Mr Belcher sprang back to the trolley and pressed the button. The propeller jerked, hesitated and then began to spin and at the same moment a blast of hot air picked up the rigger as if in an invisible hand and flung him over the trolley in the direction of the airscrew.

When consciousness returned Belcher found himself looking straight up at the propeller from where he lay on the ground. The blades were still, for by the grace of God the Merlin had not fired properly, but all that Keith could think of now was the singing in his ears and the pains in both his knees and right shoulder, while all around confusion reigned at dispersal and in the background the Spitfires of No. 64 Squadron raced over the grass to intercept the audacious raider.

What had in fact taken place was that the Hurricanes were dispersed inside the perimeter track and not in blast pens and the Dornier had dropped a stick of light bombs amongst them. When matters were finally sorted out it was the sneering NCO who had been on the receiving end of the type of thing he normally dealt out; but the last word came from the pilot, who remarked, "That's the first time I've done a twenty-degree bank in an aeroplane without leaving the ground!"

Then, suddenly, but not altogether unexpectedly, the ferocity of attacks increased as the month was waning, the target being Dover once more. Here there had been five civil warnings on the last Saturday of the month, two of them developing into raids in the afternoon, the earlier taking place at 2.30 p.m. and the next at 6 p.m., both of these attacks being directed at the Eastern Arm near the Marine Station.

A far heavier attack was delivered by the inevitable Stukas with Messerschmitt escort early in the morning of the following Monday, the same area as before as well as ships in the Camber being singled out for attention. Now it was that the repair ship *Sandhurst,* with the destroyer *Codrington* alongside, both previously damaged, was set afire and some hours after the last raider had departed, the columns of smoke that rose into the July sky could be seen for miles around as the Fire Brigade fought a blaze that was fed from the fractured oil storage tanks on the cliffs pouring their contents into the dock. *Gronland,* another victim of a previous raid, was now sunk and the yacht *Gulzar* too was lost, a pair of tugs, *Dapper* and *Snapper,* being prevented from rendering any assistance due to the barrier formed by the blazing oil. Soon after, Dover was supplied with a balloon barrage but before long these became ready targets for Messerschmitt fighters clearing the way for the bombers and the first silver leviathan was to go down on the last day of the month.

CHAPTER EIGHT

Overpower the English

On 1st August Hitler threw down the chips with his Directive No. 17: "I intend to intensify air and sea warfare against the English homeland. I therefore order . . . that the German Luftwaffe is to overpower the English Air Force with all the resources at its command", and the order concluded with the declaration that the opening date for these attacks was only four days distant, on 5th August. Hampshire alone within No. 11 Group and Somerset outside received from the air green and yellow leaflets containing the Nazi leader's "Last Appeal to Reason" that same day, and press photographers had a field-day taking pictures of civilians reading it bearing the obligatory broad grins. The same day also, Hugh Dowding issued an edict which was a testimony to the workers in the aircraft factories who had toiled in the weeks after Dunkirk until they were almost asleep at their benches; the order was to authorize the return of fighter squadron strength from sixteen to twenty machines each with two in reserve.

As if to compensate for the comparative quiet in south-eastern skies on the previous day, there was a brisk attack on yet another convoy, now that they had resumed the old sea-lanes towards the Channel, by Erprobungsgruppe 210, which was still specializing in this type of work under their Swiss-born commander, Hauptmann Walter Rubends-dörffer, who had only a fortnight more to live. The following day saw some exploratory attacks both by night and day, so even on those few days, soon to vanish altogether, when there seemed to be little activity, prisoners were taken and crashed aircraft carefully dissected by the Intelligence officers. Occasionally these encounters with the enemy could be light-hearted instead of grave and Gerhard Granz recalls the day when he had to abandon his aircraft, which came to earth on a farm at Billericay. His descent by parachute had set him down in an orchard and scarcely had he worked the harness release when his attention was caught by the sight of a pair of British steel helmets behind a hedge. "Good afternoon," called Granz. The wearers of the helmets raised their heads in relief at not being addressed in a foreign tongue, so that one of the pair called back, "Blimey, you're English. That's splendid."

"Not at all," came the reply in perfect English, "I am German!"

But if occasionally meetings such as this were sometimes cordial, they were not common, and at least one record exists of a flyer, who had reached the ground safely at a lonely Surrey golf club, being immediately murdered in a brutal manner before any witnesses had gathered or the police appeared to make a rescue.

There was certainly plenty to occupy the ground staff at RAF stations throughout the Group and the improved weather was welcome since very little work on the aircraft was now carried out in the hangars, which were regarded as too vulnerable, the greater part of maintenance being done outside. Beyond the boundaries of many such stations security demanded that Home Guards, then known as Local Defence Volunteers (LDVs) soon after the formation of that corps, could be encountered at spacings of about fifty yards about the whole perimeter of an aerodrome, maintaining patrols despite their lack of proper equipment.

As if in confirmation of Hitler's promise "Be patient *he* will come," the first days of August saw only limited activity despite a maintained improvement in the weather. This was to some extent a surprise for No. 11 Group's headquarters, which had been geared to a more immediate assault. As one of the preparations for this, many small but vital alterations had been ordered and carried out, for in the coming fight it was realized at all levels that the prize was not only the survival of the British way of life but in the longer term that of the English-speaking peoples everywhere, including the United States, and indeed civilization.

At squadron level, however, it is doubtful if there was any realization that history was being made. It was much more a case of a job of work that had to be done, as for example the intensive programme that had earlier been carried out to adapt Merlin engines for high-octane fuel in place of the lower grade originally used. This called for a change of all the sparking-plugs and adjustment of the carburettors. On the former task both fitters and riggers could be pressed into use to speed matters up, but the carburettor work was restricted to Group I tradesmen of the Maintenance Flights and all day long there was a great coming and going as fighters were taken across one at a time for the work to be carried out. Keith Belcher recalls an incident when the CO's machine, the last to be dealt with that day, was taxied across by Squadron Leader J. R. (Joe) Kayll at something like sixty miles an hour with himself as a passenger on the port tailplane. "Did you think I'd forgotten you were there?" laughed the officer on seeing the other's white face. "No, sir," came the reply, "but if I'd known it was going to be that fast a trip I'd have asked to borrow your helmet and goggles!"

Small incidents such as this help us to understand the atmosphere of the time for it was one when discipline was never enforced on duty. One airman recalls the occasion when he forgot to replace his identity disc after having a shave before going out on an evening pass. At first he was detained by a Home Guard patrol and then by one of Irish Guards until collection by Service Police. By now the time was around 12.45 a.m. but he and his companions were duly booked in as at 23.59 hours and no charge was preferred.

There was still time, but only just, for the characters larger than life to flourish, for soon even these would become wearied and sit, changed men, white-faced with fatigue in the cockpits of Hurricanes and Spitfires, leaping into activity only when the adrenalin flowed once more, stimulated by the order to scramble, perhaps over a blaring Tannoy. Before the waiting time ran out and the threatened new assault began in all its fury some of these bright spirits were able to make their strange mark on posterity therefore, and there will have been few in Sector "B" who did not know of the Canadian Flight Lieutenant, L. M. Gaunce, whose initials gave him the immediate nickname of "Elmer". One of his best-known exploits was a take-off ignoring runways straight out of a blast pen, and there were those who affirmed that the Hurricane was only coaxed to become airborne because the undercarriage was retracted at an altitude of about twelve feet.

Another tale of this same officer is less well known for it predated the Battle of Britain period, yet it typified the spirit of the men who fought in it. The time was soon before the return of the squadron from France and Gaunce had a bottle of rare French liqueur that he wished to deliver to a house in Folkestone by the practical means of dropping it in the back garden. For this, the bottle was packed in a great quantity of rag from the stores and about this was wrapped a final outer layer held in place by wax-braided cord, so that the single bottle looked finally something like a rolled-up carpet. It was only with some degree of difficulty that it would fit into the cockpit together with the pilot! Now Mr Gaunce could sideslip a Gladiator with which the squadron was equipped in those days like few others, indeed this manoeuvre was carried out so steeply that the engine became starved of air from the ram effect of forward flight and yellow flames licked out of the exhausts. This, said the pilot, was the technique he proposed to use in order to deliver the bottle and he straight away took off to do just this.

"If it didn't drop in her garden, it sure as hell went next door," the pilot told his ground crew on returning to base, but his fitter was silent for a moment, occupied with removing something from the undercarriage. "Did next door have a wireless aerial, sir?" enquired he, straightening up and displaying a length of wire complete with china insulator that he had just unwound from the port leg!

Despite a rather fearsome appearance, partly due to a somewhat scarred and swarthy complexion and a large black moustache, Gaunce was a kindly man who, whispered some, must have had shares in the confectionery business, for it was his habit to give his ground crew a Mars Bar each as they carried out their daily inspection. One of the men recalls that this "B" Flight officer at one time asked if his flying helmet could be painted bright red on the front and back panels, and this was worn with a dark anti-glare visor which would flip down in front of his goggles!

It was men such as Gaunce who took on the Nazi attackers in the Dover Strait on the early morning of 5th August and again after lunchtime, but despite the date being that on which Hitler promised fresh attacks would come, there was little sign of greater activity, indeed the command total of about four hundred sorties flown was certainly less than the later average, which was greater by as much as half again, and the same was true of the Tuesday following and the next day also.

The pace of activity showed a sharp increase as the month advanced, so much so that some historians following a pattern suggested in the official account of the summer's struggle have regarded it as the opening of a new and important phase in the fight for survival. However that may be it is certainly true that on this day took place the biggest action up to that time, it being centred off the Isle of Wight, and Winston Churchill was given minute-by-minute reports on the air fighting.

Prevailing weather of showers and bright intervals with cloud over the English Channel particularly favoured the enemy. Spitfire pilot Robinson of No. 152 Squadron on patrol over the sea remembers the day particularly well, since he and two others were bounced by the enemy as they were making for base to rearm and refuel. Training and natural pride demanded that this should be done in immaculate formation, a tradition in the battle that the majority of pilots attempted to keep no matter how tired they were. This also had the effect of keeping up civilian morale and if the approach could be followed by a spectacular "beat-up" of the station then so much the better; yet the result of these high spirits was that no one was keeping an adequate look-out for the odd marauding enemy fighter.

As if from nowhere the tracer started coming. With unerring aim it smashed into the wing of the Spitfire so that the machine could be felt to shudder under the impact. The engine too took its quota of the murderous fire and in a moment smoke began to escape in great billowing clouds from under the cowling. Strange thoughts pass through a man's mind in a situation such as this and Robinson would have been unusual if he had not been momentarily bewildered by the sudden attack out of the seemingly empty sky. The encounters with odds of fifty to twelve and the chases at wave-top height over the sea such as had been his experience over the previous few days placed him in the position of almost expecting death, but this type of thing was different.

The immediate reaction taught to pilots to extract them from a situation such as this came quickly to Robinson. He flung "N-nuts" into a half roll on to its back with a sharp movement of the rudder accompanied by a push on the control column. The dive that followed lost him some 5,000 feet and when he came out of it there was nothing left to do but to put the machine down as quickly as possible. So far he had been in luck but how long would it be before Dame Fortune failed to smile? A nice clear field below gave the opportunity sought. With careful movement of the stick now, not knowing how badly the Messerschmitt's fire had damaged the Spitfire, the pilot brought it in for some sort of an approach. Then came the moment of impact: with a shattering noise the fighter shot over the grass, the airscrew blades buckled back almost slowly. With a scream of tortured metal the port wing was sliced off at the root, before the unseen ditch caught the Spitfire for a final ignominy and pitched it up on its nose, where it remained at a crazy angle with the wing gouged deeply into the earth. Shaky and slightly dazed, Sergeant Robinson scrambled out and slid to the ground as local people, seemingly materializing from nowhere, converged on the spot, children at the run leading the way.

Strangely enough, Kent, which was to become almost the traditional place of battle while Britain fought for survival, was little affected by this new phase in the struggle centred about 11 Group. Yet despite this the Dover siren was sounded twenty times. Perhaps one reason was that the Luftwaffe chiefs were at the time preoccupied with the date of the coming *Adler Tag* the Eagle Day which was to launch the main air assault, and this, despite the declaration that Hitler had issued some time before, was finally agreed to be 10th August.

When that day dawned it turned out to be one that did not give much promise of good flying weather. There were smiles and knowing nods in the Luftwaffe messes amongst the men who had long ago termed their meteorological

officers "false prophets". Instead of the massive assault that
the day should have seen, the Channel was cloudy with few
bright periods and as a consequence Luftwaffe activity was
confined largely to reconnaissance flights and the appearance of a single Dornier 17Z over West Malling, which
dropped some eleven bombs. The Operations Rooms
meanwhile saw a number of British fighters scrambled to
investigate "X" raids, unidentified tracks so called from
their prefix to the sequence number on the plotting tables in
much the same manner as friendly fighters were designated
with a red letter "F" on a white background while confirmed raiders were identified by a black "H" (Hostile)
against yellow.

The abortive *Adler Tag* was marked by a raid by Walter
Rubendsdörffer's Erprobungsgruppe 210, although only a
handful of the twenty-eight specially selected pilots were
committed by the genial Hauptmann. The attack had been
mounted from the unit's base in the Pas de Calais using only
its Messerschmitt 110s, and although the target was in fact
the Norwich factory of Boulton Paul, the producers of the
Defiant fighters of recent unhappy memory, the raiders
appeared briefly on the plotting table of 11 Group.

As happens in Britain, the weather twenty-four hours
later had undergone a complete change and early church-
goers on this Sunday found that it was fine with blue skies
obscured by only a little mist which was soon burnt off by
the sun, although these conditions were to fade somewhat
as the day advanced.

First sortie by the enemy saw Rubendsdörffer's picked
Gruppe over Dover behind an advanced-guard of their own
single-seaters sweeping ahead to destroy the balloons trailing their dangerous cables. This was not the first time that
such had happened but the spectacular nature of these
attacks ensured that they were well publicized in the Press
of both Britain and Germany. Although only three balloons
were in fact accounted for and the seventeen following
Messerschmitt 110s released their bomb loads without

interference, it was believed that the attack was to clear the way for a force of larger bombers. The raid had been well timed in that it found the British standing patrols near to the end of their fuel and consequently at a disadvantage, while when the mistake had been realized it meant that the fighters sent off to remedy the situation were despatched too late and missed their intended quarry.

It was only ninety minutes later, at 8.30 a.m., that another attack seemed to be developing against a Channel convoy and immediately afterwards a large force of the enemy appeared with the intention of luring the British fighter squadrons into a fight over Dover. This was only partly successful since the wily Park retained sufficient fighters to counter the main attack that he felt must be coming. There was not long to wait, for the RDF stations started to register the kind of blip on their scanning cathode-ray tubes that indicated a fresh and large force of bombers approaching; this was the main raid and the target was the varied installations at Portland, but the reserve fighters were now sent in and a fierce fight began. Into this mêlée came further Messerschmitts to clear more of the balloons, these being from 961 Balloon Squadron safe-guarding Dover, but strangely the afternoon was quiet and next to no enemy activity was reported.

The following day, 11th August, Dover was the centre of a concentrated area attack covering not only the town but also the nearby fighter stations on which it relied for its defence as well as shipping in the Strait. Some two hundred enemy aircraft attacked in eleven waves, and as far as the town proper was concerned this too was the day on which the first shells from the long-range guns on the French coast fell. Elsewhere the RDF stations were singled out for con-centrated attacks and that at Ventnor on the Isle of Wight was put out of action, the coverage from this station not being restored for eleven days when Bembridge began operating.

A Spitfire pilot from No. 64 Squadron recalls the day

vividly, for this was the occasion when his unit, detailed to intercept a raid between Dungeness and Dover, flew into cloud and became separated despite the fact that the day was marked by fairly clear weather. Together with one other, the pair of Spitfires now formed a patrol on their own and it was a matter of only minutes before there loomed up in front of them a formation of almost fifty Dorniers. Despite the odds the two dived into the bombers, selecting one of the rear machines as their first victim. After a few bursts from the fighters the bomber began to show signs of fire aboard but the attack had to be broken off due to the sudden appearance of an Me 109 on the Spitfire's tail, while at the same time the return fire from one of the Dornier's gunners was striking home. The use of the standard evasive action on this occasion managed to get rid of the Messer- schmitt but the pilot decided to return to base, uncertain how much damage the machine had suffered, while in the meantime the other Spitfire pilot closed in on the Dornier and made sure that the internal fire was well alight before he too had to break off the attack.

But if matters were going badly in the south-east corner of Kent they were no better elsewhere, for the day was the one when the RDF stations were singled out for heavy attacks since it was now realized by the enemy that these were a key part of the defence system. Nevertheless, strangely, the Monday raids were never seriously repeated, so the judgement of history must be that the August day was also the one when the first fundamental mistake was made: had the RDF stations been again pounded with similar severity, the outcome of the battle over 11 Group could well have been different.

Fighter squadrons were at readiness throughout the area on this day and it was while pilots waited in their cockpits for the order to take off that the Tannoy crackled into life at Sector "B"'s main station announcing that the Distin- guished Flying Cross had been awarded to Flight Lieuten- ant Gaunce, Pilot Officer Hugo and newly engaged Flying

Officer Collard. The latter was now in a state of almost complete exhaustion, seemingly only half-awake in fact, although still managing to fly. It was this trio, in the air again within minutes of the announcement, that claimed three of the enemy shared between them, while Pilot Officer McClintock made his first kill in the form of a Dornier 17z although this was not confirmed.

With a further change in the weather, dawn broke on the following morning, 12th August, with a deep band of cloud over the greater part of south-east England at no more than 4,000 feet, yet despite this the first attacks of the long-awaited *Adler Tag* were launched, mainly in the afternoon when the weather improved. Nazi intelligence had assured the crews of the raiding bombers that the wearing attacks against convoys earlier had diminished British fighter squadrons to mere token formations and Günter Beck, flying with a Junkers 88 unit, remembers this day to have been the first one when he heard the cynical remark as 11 Group's interceptors formed up for the attack: "Here come the last half-dozen Spitfires."

Elsewhere there were strange reports by the police of parachutes being found, forty-five, so it was said, having been picked up in Derbyshire and Stafford as well as north of the Scottish border.

By now, what little professional anxiety there had been at 11 Group Headquarters was beginning to evaporate, not because at this point victory was by any means certain but more likely due to the fact that clearly the long wait was over and the RAF was at grips with the worst that could happen, and this mood of confidence increased as the attacks began to turn to the fighter fields. It was about this time too that the King and Queen began to pay occasional visits to many of the front-line stations and to headquarters and these, together with the appearance of Winston Churchill, on one occasion accompanied by his wife, were to act as a tremendous tonic for all concerned. It was after viewing the plotting table for some five minutes in silence at Group

Headquarters the following after that the Prime Minister first made the historic utterance about the "Few" which has since passed into our language, although such eloquence was not uppermost in the minds of his party, among whom Lord Ismay has since confessed himself "sick with fear" at what he saw unfolding before him.

Now the battle raged on in earnest although the number of sorties flown by the Luftwaffe was fewer than had been mounted on 13th August, and it was on this day that No. 615 Squadron lost not only Pilot Officer "Monty" Montgomery, but also the weary Flying Officer Collard. Just how he met his death has never been fully explained, for on that Wednesday he was acting the unenvied role of "tail-weaver" ("arse end Charlie") and was lost with no one seeing his demise. It was not until the next day that it was announced that a body had been found and identified, a fact that "Sammy" Samson records in his diary together with the loss on 15th August of Sergeant D. W. Halton flying "B", P2801, which crashed and burnt out at Seal just after midday.

The pace and ferocity of the attacks mounted on that day are well known, including as they did the attack by Erprobungsgruppe 210 on Croydon Aerodrome seeking, some claimed at the time, Biggin Hill or Kenley, an attack that cost the leader his life. The Messerschmitt 110 that formed the spearhead of the raid had come in over Weybridge, so that no warning was sounded for the civil population, although the story of the time that dive-bombing had been adopted was untrue. Eye-witnesses confirm that it was normal flat-trajectory bombing, but "dive-bombing" was the latest phrase and tended to be applied to any attack. "Severe casualties," records Samson in his diary of the time, "factory razed; excellent dog fights as Spits and Hurries engage Jerries."

Elsewhere in the area Brendan E. (Paddy) Finucane had joined No. 65 Squadron at Hornchurch as a Pilot Officer and claimed to have shot down a Messerschmitt 109 two days earlier. Although he was to receive tremendous publicity in the British Press at a later date with the award of the DSO and two bars to his DFC, some "Regulars" of the time do not remember him with undue affection, regarding him as dictatorial.

Although the true heat of battle had raged for only a short time the countryside within 11 Group in particular was becoming littered, it seemed, with wrecked Nazi aircraft, much publicized in the newspapers with a consequent boost to civilian morale. So much so in fact that the columns of *Punch* summed the situation up with a cartoon where a local was giving directions to a visitor merely by the reference points of crashed aircraft. Occasionally the grim sight of an aeroplane crashing was to be witnessed by small numbers of civilians who would have been better off under cover, and indeed more than one newspaper was shortly to publish a front-page feature complaining of crowds of "Bank Holiday proportions" under a headline which complained: "Too Many People Are Staying in Streets during Raids", adding that ". . . the police have no power to compel people to take cover. The position is that if you want to be foolish you are not prevented by law."

In the countryside the chances of such behaviour proving fatal were reduced and on the border of the group area on 15th August, Mr Gregory Fry recalls the sight of a couple of bombers' ends in these words:

It was about 5 o'clock in the afternoon, and there had been a raid against Portsmouth and Southampton, and a Junkers 88 suddenly appeared from the direction of the latter at a height of, I should think, only about a couple of thousand feet, with, hotly in pursuit two British fighters firing at it as they came, diving in from each side and firing bursts as they did so. Then as we were watching, another plane appeared out of the blue about a mile away and came streaking down in flames to hit the ground over the hill perhaps a mile and a half away to that a column of smoke went up. Almost simultaneously the plane that had flown over first climbed slightly and two or three parachutes opened as some of the crew baled out, and then the machine glided down again, to disappear behind some trees.

Being a Home Guard, I went indoors for my forage cap—we had no rifles in those days, and made off towards the column of smoke, and together with one or two other people I met on the way were soon walking through a copse where there were bits and pieces of aircraft and human beings scattered over the bushes. As we came out of the trees, there in front of us we could see a large crater in the ground, still smoking with more bits and pieces scattered all around, while a couple of hundred yards away in a barley field was a second Junkers 88. It had obviously belly-landed, and by the time we got there the crew had evidently been taken prisoner, the three that had managed to bale out and the pilot that had managed to make a landing.

Mr Fry obviously had no camera with him then but was very keen to photograph the bomber despite the war-time restrictions on taking photographs even if one could get a film. However, he had a reel in his camera and next day went back to the site, which was guarded by an Australian sentry who stopped any pictures being taken. Nevertheless, Mr Fry was determined and managed to take a quick snap unobserved.

It is interesting to record that such was the spirit of the time that when the film was ready for collection from the developing chemist, the owner received a summons instead to the local police station, and later still the tale ended in a fine of ten shillings (50p), although the Bench agreed to keep the picture until after the war! A request for its return after VE day, five years later, brought the print back after a few days' delay, and it is reproduced in this book.

No one has up to now discovered the identities of the crew who perished in the first machine, which was from II/LG1, but those of the second, reportedly brought down by Flight Lieutenant Hope and Sergeant Guy, both of No. 601 Squadron, are known to have been Oberleutnant Suin de Boutemard, Unteroffizier Weigang, Oberfeldwebel Grund and Feldwebel Luder. The aircraft was a II Gruppe Stab machine as shown by its codes, L1+SC, indicating that this one too came from LG1.

The business of picking up crews from crashed aircraft

was always something of a problem. On land it could be performed by the police, LDVs or Army, whether the men to be taken were British or German. Over the sea, the RNLI and the Royal Navy were chiefly responsible for men rescued from home waters, although beyond the normal territorial waters the Luftwaffe had quite an efficient air-sea rescue service, compared to that of the RAF which was at the time comparatively primitive.

However, there could have been few stranger deliverences than that reported on the same day as the two Junkers machines already described were brought down, for on this occasion the rescue was performed by a young girl, Peggy Prince, who lived on the Channel coast. It was twenty minutes to six in the morning when a tremendous beating on the door of her home woke her and her family, who were told by two soldiers that an aircraft was down in the water about two miles out to sea. The reason for their choice of household to rouse was because there was kept almost the last boat in the district, a ten-foot clinker-built canoe.

Since she did not know the two men nor have any knowledge of their seamanship, Miss Prince insisted on going along, despite being warned that in all likelihood the men to be rescued were enemy, and against any bid to take advantage of her, one of the soldiers took along his rifle.

It was first necessary to carry the boat over three barriers of barbed wire and a concrete wall before going down a ladder to the beach so that by the time the boat was launched the aeroplane had sunk.

The first trip found no survivors and since the canoe was leaking, Miss Prince turned back, only to be told by watchers on the beach that three figures could be made out a little further from the spot, swimming in the water. A second trip was made, this time with only one of the soldiers, and overhead a Hurricane fighter provided escort to lead the girl towards the right spot. On reaching this she picked up an RAF sergeant, the aeroplane being British and not German while a fishing boat picked up the remaining pair. The sergeant later gallantly declared that he chose to be rescued by the occupant of the canoe and dived out of sight when the look-out from the fishing boat seemed to be looking in his direction!

CHAPTER NINE

The Heat of August

As August moved into its second half it was not only the sunshine that increased. So too did the heat of battle. By now it was evident that this was the long-awaited crisis that had been expected since the fall of France and the evacuation from Dunkirk. In order to keep abreast with the situation, not only Keith Park but also his deputy, Gerald Gibbs, were in the habit of making unannounced visits to fighter stations in the Group and as personal transports a couple of Hawker Hurricanes were kept at readiness by the Station Flight, Northolt. At this particular time Fighter Command as a whole had on strength 283 Spitfires, 533 Hurricanes and 54 Blenheim fighters, plus 30 Defiants and 5 Gladiator biplanes. To the total must be added those machines temporarily unserviceable but which would be ready within twelve, or at the most twenty-four hours. Such planes accounted for the majority of single-seaters, and brought the grand total of strength up to slightly over one thousand machines.

One factor of RAF organization to which there was a tendency at this time was to place the technical backing at fighter stations on what has been termed a "factory" basis, with the demands of service and maintenance given greater priority than the military aspect, that is to say the organization of small units under a single, well-known and technically skilled officer, and this was one of the changes which were wisely thought to be immediately called for by Sir Keith Park's Senior Air Staff Officer. It is still comparatively little known that it was at just this moment that Park was suddenly taken ill and was on sick leave for about a fortnight, so that it was on the shoulders of Gerald Gibbs that the entire responsibility for the command of 11 Group fell during this period.

Another innovation ordered now was that trenches be dug alongside the dispersal points where the ground crews, described by the same senior officer as "heroic", could take cover, thus enabling them to carry on until the last moment when that particular target was attacked. The same idea was also behind the change of policy with regard to unexploded bombs. Hitherto these had been flagged and aircraft were forbidden to pass within a certain distance of where they lay on airfields—a policy that was preventing fighters getting away to intercept further raids. This was therefore altered and instead of the former arrangement that could on occasion put out of action perhaps a complete airfield, all restrictions on aircraft movement were relaxed in the light of the expressed fact that a bomb is active for only a single, unknown split-second of time.

Although the *average* number of sorties flown by the RAF by now has already been expressed by many historians to be in the region of six hundred, in fact this total could by mid-August be as high as one thousand. The enemy average total was perhaps 350, although the operations flown by the Luftwaffe on 15th August came to the startling total of 1,800!

"B" Sector was alerted early in the afternoon of 16th August when the civilian warning was sounded at 12.45 p.m. but although raiders were heard they were not visible from the ground and the targets on that day were away from the centre of the sector at such places as Wimbledon in south London. Elsewhere the picture was very different. The first intimation of the pending attack on Tangmere came after midday when the RDF screens showed a large raid approaching the important 11 Group Sector Station, and further reports indicated that the formation consisted of Junkers 87, Stukas. Up to now the enemy activity had been comparatively light and before 11 a.m. there had been a singular absence of hostile tracks on the plotting tables. The squadrons based at Tangmere during this period were Nos 43 and 601, which used nearby Westhampnett, base for 145 Squadron, as a satellite airfield.

A witness just outside the perimeter fence recalls the tremendous noise of the attack. He had to cover his ears as wave after wave of Stukas from Fliegerkorps VIII screamed down to deliver their bombs and, whether they were using their wind-driven sirens or not, a device which added terror to the diving attacks, the crescendo of sound which was added to by the roar and boom of the exploding bombs was such that, despite stopped ears, he was driven almost to physical sickness by the sound. Strangely, the raid was of short duration so that it ceased as quickly as it had begun but when the dazed men on the ground emerged from what cover they had been able to find not only did the smell of burning come to their nostrils from the huge fires sending up great billowing clouds of black smoke, but there was also the stench of cordite and dust hanging in the air. Every one of the hangars received hits.

The Hurricanes of the three resident squadrons had been scrambled relatively early but they had not been able to gain sufficient height when the bombers struck. "I couldn't see the Stukas at first," wrote a diarist afterwards, "because they just materialized out of the glaring sun and came belting down to fling little black things before they pulled up and were away. I was too terrified trying to keep alive myself to think properly, but only some of these black objects, which must have been bombs, blew up. With others, just nothing happened, it was uncanny." In fact these were delayed-action bombs and the rest of the day and part of the night were punctuated by explosions as the bombs went off.

In the encounter between the defenders and the attacking bombers which followed, the Hurricanes were joined by Spitfires from No. 602 Squadron, which seemed to fling themselves at the escorting Messerschmitts, leaving the Hurricanes to deal with the Junkers, four of those from 3/StG2 being brought down.

The first of these that failed to return to its base at St Omer was one crewed by Unteroffiziers Obergefr and Linse, both of whom were killed when the machine came screaming down over Honor Farm, at Sidlesham. It was soon joined by another which may have been guided in for an attempted landing in the fields beside the Selsey to Chichester road, but if this is the case then the pilot failed in his intention, for the bomber came to a halt in a hedge beside the road having ripped off its undercarriage with the impact, moments before. The crew was captured.

Less lucky was the pair in the machine that was lost in the Channel after limping for some way out to sea, while the fourth came down on land at South Mundham, and although reports agree that the gunner was killed, some state that the pilot escaped albeit seriously injured.

It seemed therefore that Tangmere had been reduced to little more than ashes, for even after the fires had been finally damped down it required only a casual inspection to see the extent of the other damage. Pipes and masonry lay in fearful confusion, all windows were reduced to nothing more than wicked splinters which accounted for some of the deaths, and there had been many injuries, including that to the station commander, who staggered about still slightly dazed, attempting to attend to his duties while the blood ran from his face wound. Yet despite all this the station was, by dint of massive work in a seemingly impossible situation by everyone present, back in commission some eight hours later.

The ordeal of 11 Group, which had suffered attacks over a large part of Sussex and Kent at the same time, was mirrored in the following morning's newspapers, which claimed that the RAF had accounted for sixty-nine of the previous day's raiders, including those which had penetrated the defences as far as the "south-western suburbs of London" which were raided for the first time that night, adding that the booking hall of a railway station, a church, houses, two stores, a club and a garage had all been hit.

Meanwhile the raids of the previous day had been seized by the Nazi radio for an exercise in propaganda that at the time had a certain air of novelty about it, for Radio Bremen was interrupted when the announcer stated that "A report has just been received that the first squadron has almost reached harbour works of the River Thames. A second wave of bombers is now over the Channel"; later the official Air Ministry communiqué dismissed the attack on Tangmere with the words: "An RAF aerodrome was attacked", before going on to claim that eleven of the raiding Junkers were shot down by fighters, although the wording was careful in retaining just sufficient ambiguity to permit several interpretations and thus confuse the enemy. There was added a rider, though, that must have surprised more than one reader in enemy territory who might have a source of supply through neutral countries when he read the tale of the station commander who owed his life to the glimpse in his rear-view mirror of what was claimed to be a Heinkel 113 diving on his Hurricane's tail. In fact the type was never used over the British Isles throughout that summer's fighting although an examination of the now yellowing combat reports in official archives shows several references to these fighters being "identified".

But if the announcement by Radio Bremen had made good use of the daylight raids as a subject for graphic word-pictures, other radio stations described the somewhat light attacks after dark in rather more lurid terms, stating that "With infernal howling, great detonations and sheets of flame lit up the district south of Barking. Air raid alarm on air raid alarm, the howling of sirens and the thunder of guns are in London."

In the United States too the air battles of mid-August were front-page news, one reporter describing the country as "blanketed with anxiety over the capital's plight" below such headlines in heavy type as "Great Airfight Above London". The reports were all totally inaccurate since Britain kept America waiting for her side of the story, so reporters across the Atlantic had only Nazi sources to draw upon. Nevertheless, some of the observations were prophetic and summed the situation up in a manner that historians since have failed to do, an example of this appearing in the *New York Times* which read: "If this is a new Trafalgar or the 1940 version of Waterloo, the extraordinary fact is that the RAF, outnumbered by the Germans, still holds the control of the air over Britain." Even nearer the mark was the *New York Sun,* which commented: "Britain is making a gallant stand, so brave and effective that many observers predict that invasion by large forces of troops will never happen."

Writers such as these were not alone in their accurate prophesy, for the Samson diary had this to say on the uneventful Saturday, 17th August: "Very quiet day. Is this the calm before the storm? No Jerry activity." The reason for the calm puzzled many, for the weather continued fine yet the Luftwaffe activity over No. 11 Group was confined to reconnaissance flights by individual aircraft and the British fighters which were despatched to form convoy protection made no contact with the enemy. Pilots such as James Lacey, flying 501 Squadron Hurricanes out of Kenley and lately at Croydon, which had the previous day encountered a mixed gaggle of nearly forty Messerschmitts and Dorniers strung out along the coast between Dungeness and Hastings, were able now to relax temporarily and take refuge in sleep to restore the ravaged reflexes that had been so severely tried in the previous hectic days.

Sunday, 18th August, broke with the promise of a magnificent, golden day, one remembers, although this was to be kept only locally, for in some areas the skies clouded over by lunchtime. It had been the intention of the Nazis to erase the fighter arm of the Royal Air Force in a single week, a not altogether impossible hope, but this had met with failure so that, in order to keep matters to the planned schedule, this final day with its good flying weather was to be devoted to just this aim, although the day was well advanced before the first hostile plots denoting massed raids began slowly to creep across the table of the Group Operations Room.

The chief raid suddenly materialized for the area when it was realized that this was to be a strike at the heart, quite literally, of the fighting area that was south-east England. The alarm was given at the Kenley sector station at about 1 p.m. or a little later, and what is remembered as "hordes of Jerry kites" was in fact a two-pronged attack, with one formation at a considerably lower altitude than the others. Three squadrons could have been available from the sector, but No. 615 had no chance to defend their traditional home (which had given a meaning to their Hurricanes' squadron code letters of "KW" as meaning "Kenley Warriors"), for this unit was away countering a simultaneous attack over Hawkinge. Only No. 64 Squadron Spitfires were left to cope with the high-level attack from Kenley itself, while the Hurricanes of 111 Squadron from neighbouring Croydon were to deal with the nine raiders at the lower altitude, although the latter had a grave disadvantage in that they were too close to the target before battle was joined and therefore without the advantage of any superior height.

The ensuing fight which raged on the Sunday afternoon was one of the most savage that had been fought so near

London up to that time and despite heavy anti-aircraft fire that had to wait until the raiders had cleared trees and roof-tops before they could be fired upon. Apart from this fire, which was very intense, the Parachute and Cable device (PAC) was also used and policeman George Lee recalled for the author the tale against himself in which he failed to recognize the descending parachutes for what they were and instead took them to be large numbers of distant parachutists, and took the appropriate action!

The raid was short and certainly sharp with civilians recalling with great clarity even at this distance in time the sight of Dorniers at zero height over the neighbouring town of Caterham-on-the-Hill. The raiders descended so low that the details of the national markings and even the facial expressions of the crews could be made out from the ground.

All the hangars except one were to suffer direct hits and Flight Lieutenant Cromie was killed in an air-raid shelter. Perhaps the most tragic and ironical occurrence was that which culminated in Reg Cunningham staggering into the blast-pen-cum-shelter, white-faced and covered in blood. The sight that greeted him here was not likely to give him much confidence for several of the men taking cover had thrown themselves on the floor to lie there with caps stuffed into mouths waiting, as one afterwards remembered, "for the one with our name on it". The turn of events which led up to this were as follows.

Cunningham had been in the Flight lorry when the "Attack Alarm" had been given in company with a Regular from "A" Flight, a 22-year-old from the North, 617220 Leading Aircraftman T. Holroyd, who had been given the unfortunate nickname of "Doom" due to his pessimistic outlook. Despite the savagery of the attack he had asked Cunningham to change places with him as he was always keen to drive the vehicle. This Cunningham agreed to do and a matter of moments later the lorry was caught in the hail of fire from a ground-strafing rear gunner of a Dornier,

Holroyd being killed instantly with a bullet through the head. It was his blood that had washed over the terrified Cunningham who had staggered into the shelter.

But the day had its happier stories too, for Pilot Officer "Dutch" Hugo survived a fearful encounter with the enemy and baled out although wounded, as did the redoubtable and reckless "Elmer" Gaunce, who had a reputation for having force-landed more Hurricanes than any other pilot in his squadron. On this occasion he had been severely mauled in an engagement with the raiders so that he had to bale out over Godstone, Surrey, although this particular incident in no way compared with an earlier exploit when he had been forced to abandon his fighter at more than 20,000 feet. He then did a delayed drop through the fighting aircraft below and landed in a tree. This made his return from this particular sortie overdue but he suffered only a scratch on the nose!

Yet the day also had further tragic events to tell of, for this was the occasion when Peter Walley, one of the founder members of the original 615 Squadron, to whom a memorial plaque now graces the wall of Merton Technical College, was to die. On the previous day he had been telling another member of the unit that he disagreed with the interception tactics then being used and that he would soon be submitting his own ideas for consideration. The opportunity for these views to be presented never came for the next day at 1.30 p.m., P. K. Walley, the twenty-year-old sergeant who was soon to be commissioned, fell to the guns of a Messerschmitt 109 and finally crashed to his death at Morden. A resident of the time remembers that in the more rural area that was Morden Park Golf Course then the Hurricane ploughed into a little copse of which a few of the trees remain.

From the MT (Mechanical Transport) Section, Driver Bill Jones takes up the tale: "When I arrived, the mortuary attendants with their long gloves covering the upper arm were down the crater and lifting out and into sacks what was left of the pilot. Also down there was the engine, in the hole that it had gouged out as the Hurricane hurtled down; it was all collected by 46 Maintenance Unit." A matter of a few miles away there were other wrecks, two of them at Carshalton of Hurricanes that had collided, belly to belly, when attacking what was reportedly a Heinkel 111.

Not only the operational side of Kenley suffered that day for destroyed also were some of the 18- and 30-hundred-weight trucks used to take the pilots to dispersal in company with the occasional Standard. Destroyed also was a set of coaches and thereafter three Leylands were hired from a private contractor. Among the other vehicles, mainly Albion trucks and ambulances, a survivor was the commanding officer's Humber Snipe, which was fitted with a loudspeaker for use during airfield tours, and the demands of the time also made sure that a rifle was carried on the back seat. Even the individual members of the MT were armed in those days with Smith and Wessons, remembers Jones, and "stand to" took place twice a day, half an hour before dawn and thirty minutes after dusk, the times when paratroops were particularly expected.

Elsewhere in 11 Group it was also a dreadful day and Ford, the Naval air station, was attacked. There the oil tanks were set alight, sending great columns of black billowing smoke into the summer sky.

But if those on the ground were under stress on this, the Group's most historic day to date, what was it like for the men actually aloft and involved in the killing? "Robbie" Robinson of 152 Squadron made his first kill that day, one doubly of note since it was a notorious Stuka he brought down, a type thereafter used less. He had to throttle back to avoid overshooting, and "went straight into the sea in a fountain of spray".

On the other side, Herr Schmidt remembers the day when his Junkers 87 almost shared a similar fate, the target being the RAF station on Thorney Island, and by way of preparation the unit had moved to the Cherbourg district, which offered a more convenient base. Take-off on 18th August was at 2.30 p.m. and the formation climbed to await its escort of Messerschmitt 109s. A little later he reported that the target had been identified under a beautiful summer sky and the aircraft strung out to commence the attack. "Then, quite by chance I looked round and out of the sun was approaching a 'vic' of British fighters, heading in our direction!" The next moment Schmidt was aware of a colleague going down into the sea past his cabin window, "like a flaming torch", while the other Junkers ahead made their dives.

Then it was his own turn and having first "made a wing waggle" he closed the radiator, adjusted the reflector sight and opened the ventilators to prevent the windscreen misting up. The altitude for pull-out of the dive was set on a special altimeter and now the only view was downwards with the target an enlarging toy viewed through the aiming window underneath. The motor was throttled back and the lowered dive-brakes had taken effect as the Stuka went screaming down through twelve thousand feet, its angle guided by the painted lines on the side of the transparent canopy. As a hangar appeared in the sight, he pulled the aircraft out and the bomb went automatically on its way.

His next thought was to get home to the safety of France as quickly as possible, but as he scanned the water below, as if boding ill to come, his eyes lighted on the wreckage of another aircraft tossed on the waves. But in an instant some extra sense made Schmidt turn, to see death in the form of a Spitfire on the Junkers' tail. "I had to react swiftly; mere turning would not have rid me of him so, although it was a difficult thing for the Junkers to do, I side-slipped and when I recovered the Spitfire had gone."

Not sure if his machine had been hit, Schmidt set a new course for base, worried by the lack of response from the gunner behind, but even as he did so the same Spitfire or another came on again! The same manoeuvre worked a second time and the Spitfire went harmlessly past while at

156 1940: The Story of No. 11 Group

the same moment another Stuka vanished into the sea in a flurry of foam. A moment later another Spitfire appeared. Using the same trick, but dangerously now for he was so low that the wing tip seemed to touch the water, he hoped for the best, but this time it failed to work and the hot metal from the eight Brownings could be felt jarring into the bomber. Yet, once again, the frenzied evasive action shook off the attacker before he could administer the kill.

Back over France, Schmidt felt that all he wanted was to get down, but another surprise awaited him for the landing was rough as the undercarriage, largely shot away, collapsed under the strain, leaving the Junkers to scream to a halt at the extreme end of the runway. Suddenly he was aware of running feet and gentle hands extracting his gunner, who groaned from his wounds as he was lowered on to a stretcher and rushed to hospital. It was a black day indeed for the unit as the gunner died a few days later and a comparison of notes in the Mess later showed that only one of the raiders had escaped without damage.

The following day, Hermann Göring saw fit to issue an order exhorting his men to greater effort, for time was running out and the High Command seemed to be ignorant of a fact that the aircrews knew, namely that although the attacks were certainly intensive locally, the constant re-appearance of what in the now accepted phrase was still called the "last half-dozen Spitfires" indicated an enemy that was seemingly invincible. Göring said, "We have reached the decisive period of the air war against England. The vital task is to defeat the enemy air force. Our aim is to destroy the enemy's fighters."

In the air, the following day was largely spent in sending reconnaissance aircraft to obtain reports on the previous day's attacks and the same is true of the following Tuesday and Wednesday when there was only small enemy activity. It was therefore not until Saturday, 24th August, that the bombing campaign was resumed with any savagery although the pressure had never completely relaxed so that the few who kept diaries noted how the faces of their fellows had now taken on a worn-out hue and the laughter had gone together with the spring from their step. The renewed heavy attacks of 24th August once again struck 11 Group and those in the afternoon were to include one at the RAF station of Manston in the heart of Kent, so that one may see this as marking the beginning of a new phase of operations, since a heavy raid also took place against Portsmouth this day.

The attack on the Kent airfield was mounted a short time after noon when the RDF screens showed a large formation of aircraft on course for the base. Observers confirmed this and identified the formation as consisting of twenty Junkers 88s with a heavy concentration of escorting Messerschmitt 109s. These were drawn from 2/JG51 and 6/JG51 based in the St Omer district. Since there had been an earlier attack on Ramsgate only a little more than half an hour before, the defences were ready and a vicious barrage from the anti-aircraft guns greeted the raiders.

It was now that an extraordinary decision was taken. Despite the earlier experience by the Defiant two-seaters of No. 141 Squadron, those from No. 264 based at Hornchurch were flung into the battle. These fared no better than had the earlier unit and also lost their commanding officer, who was last seen on the tail of a Junkers 88 heading out over the Channel and is presumed to have fallen into the sea and been drowned, for neither Squadron Leader Philip Hunter, DSO, nor his gunner were ever seen again.

The fight was in the main over the region of the Isle of Thanet and despite the confusion and the inadequacies of the Defiant as an interceptor, No. 264 Squadron claimed three victories for a loss of an equal number of their own.

Yet, despite events such as these—and the attack on Manston although typical was not alone—the real point of that twenty-four hours of bombing was to come after the fall of dusk; the renewal of the attacks on the defence aerodromes was to be expected, for North Weald and

Hornchurch had also suffered, but a pointer to the things that were to come was evident when about one hundred bombers droned over Sussex, Kent and Surrey, where they met little opposition, towards London itself, the focal point of the raids being in the City. It seemed as if this was part of a concerted plan, but this was not so and indeed within the Luftwaffe there were some grave pronouncements about the outcome of such a measure. The reactions were not long in coming; for only a slightly smaller force of RAF bombers was almost immediately despatched to raid the German capital of Berlin. What happened after is part of history but it should never be forgotten that although Bomber Command was not a part of the system commanded by 11 Group, which was a Fighter Command responsibility, it made a large contribution to the final outcome of the Battle of Britain.

However, at the time it seemed as if the raid on London was an integral part of the strategy for, of the fortnight that Hitler had granted to Hermann Göring to clear the RAF from the skies, only three days remained. A round-the-clock offensive had been ordered in a bid, the outcome of which was still in the balance, to achieve this mastery of the air so essential for an invasion attempt.

The War Cabinet had not been consulted before the raid on Berlin was ordered, the fact that it had taken place being merely announced at the first available meeting, which was held on the following Monday. However, it was generally approved in the light of the fact that the same day saw the continuation of the Luftwaffe attacks on the sector stations, in concert with night sorties which were now "creating problems", as Dowding was to put it in his report to the Air Ministry, adding that Hawker Hurricanes seemed to be the most likely single-seater suitable to meet the new menace, as shown by "an occasional fortunate encounter".

Tuesday, 27th August, was an historic day for several reasons, perhaps because the decision announced in Nazi Germany that Hitler was considering a prolonged

programme of attacks, even at the expense of putting back
the invasion plans, shows that the chance of launching a
cross-Channel strike did not exist only in English minds.
Adjustments were now considered called for and the front
was narrowed by the exclusion of Lympne Bay, but this was
balanced by an extension in the other direction to include
Bognor Regis and Folkestone, the latter being severely
bombed on that day.

As August drew towards its close the attacks showed no
sign of diminishing nor did the RAF seem to be being
beaten. The nature of the raids was never of the type which
could still have brought No. 11 Group to its knees, but a
serious attack was the raid carried out on 31st August
against Biggin Hill Sector Station. This was one of the few
occasions when the Junkers 88, the medium twin-engined
bomber type, was employed as a tactical, low-level strike
machine, a role for which it was admirably suited although
not anticipated in the specification issued at the design
stage. The first instance of this type of operation had taken
place on 11th August but now a formation of only nine such
machines that roared over the Kent countryside at 6 p.m.
managed to cause extensive damage and inflict casualties
out of all proportion to the small number of aircraft
employed, and the same was true of a similar attack,
mounted at the same hour on the following day. In fact the
Luftwaffe never realized the effect that sorties of this nature
was capable of having on the defence system as a whole.
Had low-level strikes been employed instead of the
attempts at saturation bombing, the outcome of the Battle of
Britain could well have been quite different.

It was this same day that saw thrown into the action No. 1
Canadian Squadron, although they were by no means in-
experienced since their base had been Croydon on the day
that an attack by Erp 210 had meant getting a dozen
Hurricanes off between the falling bombs. Now it was past
5.30 p.m. and their quarry was a formation of fifty or so
bombers with an escort high above, and waiting to pounce,

of Messerschmitt 109s. With the sun behind them the Canadians had the advantage and just as the formation was about to go in to yells of "Tally-ho" over the R/T, anti-aircraft fire erupted in between the Hurricanes and the enemy. Instead of a beam attack, therefore, the formation turned to escape the bursting shells and come in more from the rear, although the advantage of the position relative to the sun was lost. Suddenly the two formations broke up into a series of savage individual encounters and the leader, attempting to get a bead on a bomber whose rear gunner was giving as good as he got, was vaguely aware that his companion flying No. 2 was going down seemingly out of control. A second or two later, Flight Lieutenant McGregor felt no response as his gloved thumb tightened on the gun button at the top of the control column, so that discretion being the better part of valour, the leader flung his machine over and set course for home and further ammunition.

Meanwhile part of the remaining formation was having trouble with the anti-aircraft fire, the gunners below evidently mistaking the Hurricanes for some sort of Messerschmitt, but at 25,000 feet, the No. 3 managed to break free and head straight for the bombers which were still in sight. In front loomed a Dornier squarely in the Canadian's sights and calling for no deflection, the pilot evidently being unaware of the other's presence. The fighter pilot squeezed the gun button and a stream of fire smashed into the bomber. The effect was amazing and the Dornier with smoke pouring from it went down in a long arc to crash into the sea off the Kent coast.

Ten of the twelve Hurricanes were left after almost forty-five minutes in the air but the formation had been scattered by the gunners below so individual hunts were to take place. One pilot, Flying Officer Little, suddenly saw a Nazi single-seater in front and giving full deflection pumped in a long burst. In a trice the Messerschmitt seemed to fall to pieces, first the undercarriage dropped down and smoke with wicked little flames at the base began to pour from under the cowling. Then the hood flew off, careering back past the Hurricane in an almost leisurely manner, and the last sight that Little had of his victim was that of the pilot attempting to turn the machine over to make his escape by parachute.

CHAPTER TEN

Eye of the Storm

For many the Battle of Britain in No. 11 Group is
synonymous with the month of September, which opened
with fine weather. The Luftwaffe took advantage of this and
raids of large proportions were resumed on the fighter
stations. Such a policy was no doubt dictated by the
announcement by the Wehrmacht's commander, two days
before, that 15th September was to be the target date for the
invasion of the British Isles, these being the final instructions although they contained the provision that the ultimate assault would depend on "the political situation",
perhaps a reference to a still cherished hope that the British
people would demand an armistice where Nazi Germany
would be able to dictate the terms, as in France.

What was in fact happening was that the Battle of Britain
was entering a new phase that was critical despite all that
had gone before. On the same day as the instructions were

issued, the RDF stations had been showing their crops of
"blips" indicating raiders assembling shortly before 9 a.m.,
while a sinister sign was reported from across the Channel
by one British reconnaissance machine when the pilot
reported eighteen invasion barges newly arrived at Ostend.
The pilots of No. 11 Group were now beginning to suffer
greater fatigue than had ever been experienced, and today
the survivors agree that all attempts to recreate the
atmosphere of the terrible days of 1940 fail because the
weariness factor is never fully stressed. However that may
be, those at "Readiness" on the morning of Sunday, 15th
September were about to be scrambled to intercept massed
formations totalling only a little under five hundred aircraft
which set course across Dover en route for attacks on docks
in the Thames Estuary and at Eastchurch, although the
lion's share of the attention was to go forward to pound the
important RAF station at Biggin Hill, the nerve centre of
Sector C. Meanwhile "Hell's Corner" waited for what
might come in that direction, mindful of the previous day
when eighteen of the defending balloons had been
accounted for by about a dozen Messerschmitts, identified
by bright yellow noses, so that five balloons had been
hauled down to preserve them from the wasp-like
attackers.-

Quite suddenly it seemed Biggin Hill was the centre of a
concentrated attack, the sixth which it had suffered in the
space of three days. The runways were so damaged that the
station became unserviceable until late in the afternoon,
with the result that resident No. 79 Squadron's Hurricanes
had to be diverted to Croydon, where one witness recalls
their landing taking the form of "just flopping down on the
grass, irrespective of the wind direction, wherever there
was a bit of space".

As the afternoon advanced the worn-out fighter pilots of
11 Group and elsewhere were called on again to drive back a
persistent enemy, and although the spirits of the young
RAF men were indomitable they were now mostly fighting

the physical strain which was proving almost too much. Detling, Lympne and Hawkinge all came in for determined attacks together with Hornchurch, where three fighters taking off were caught by part of a stick of bombs. In a moment, where there had been a trio of graceful machines tearing down the runway there was chaos. One of the fighters that caught the worst of the blast was blown completely out of the airfield, although the pilot emerged to report back after being missing for two hours. The second machine was sent spinning like a toy across the aerodrome on its back although the pilot got off with minor injuries, and the third fighter was set alight and burned like a beacon for some time in mid-field.

It was now clear that Hugh Dowding was faced with a serious dilemma, for although there was now an undeniable atmosphere of quiet confidence at the Priory, many remember, if this type of attack was to continue it would clearly be impossible to defend the capital from south of the Thames. Then as the afternoon advanced, Biggin Hill was attacked again with renewed damage to the runways, the armoury being set alight and, most serious of all, the Sector Operations Room demolished and put out of action. Control had to be transferred to the emergency room about half a mile away, although this took a little time to effect despite the efforts of the civilian Post Office engineers who worked for hours, cold, in danger of their lives from fractured gas mains and unexploded bombs, and without food.

Monday brought more disquieting news, for the barge count opposite No. 11 Group's southern front had increased to eighty and reports were to hand that the preparations for troop embarkation were increasing at many harbours. Air superiority over Sussex and Kent now lay delicately in the balance, in part due to insufficient numbers of fresh, experienced pilots. This meant that the beaches where troops would be put ashore might have to go undefended, and the Tiger Moth biplanes and Magister trainers hastily converted as last-ditch ground-attack machines would have to be sent in on what would be for all practical purposes suicide missions if the invasion fleet set out to sea.

The Luftwaffe attacks that marked the day were designed to put the maximum strain to the point of self-destruction on the resources of 11 Group. The reconnaissance flights that had by now become an accepted part of each day's pattern were replaced by bombing attacks from quite early with formations of perhaps seventy or more bombers simultaneously pounding Biggin Hill again, together with Eastchurch, North Weald and Rochford. A combat report recalls the sort of thing that went on that fine, warm morning. A Flight of Hurricanes that had been scrambled from Kenley, to which they had only recently shifted from Gravesend, was being vectored on to a formation of Dornier 215 bombers when they were suddenly bounced by the escorting Messerschmitts. One of these was distinguished by a red cowling and this was the fighter that one of the Hurricane pilots selected as his victim, yet a moderate burst of fire seemed to have no effect so the attack was broken off for a moment, the enemy turning in the meantime. This placed him in a better position for the British pilot, who put in a long burst. Evidently the damage done was more than could be seen in the whirling confusion of combat and the Nazi pilot was seen to fling back his hood and hurl himself over the side dropping through the mêlée for almost five thousand feet before deploying his canopy.

Defeat for Great Britain by Nazi Germany was very near at this time, a fact that seems to have been realized in enemy circles also, for the High Command was to state on the following day: "The earliest day for the sailing of the invasion fleet has been fixed as 20th September and that of the landing for the twenty-first."

In Whitehall the gravity of the situation was also known, for at the same time a directive was issued to the War Cabinet ordering them to gather in the War Room if a "Red" alert, indicating imminent invasion, was received before a meeting. The assumption was that there would be sufficient time to conclude the deliberations first, while that this was no idle fear is illustrated by the barge count for twenty-four hours later, which showed the total to be 205. In addition to this it was plain from reconnaissance photographs that the Luftwaffe was currently preparing fresh airfields in northern France, while reports from espionage sources made it clear that despite the continuation of the bombing attacks on south-east England, certain units were being redeployed on these hastily set up stations. Heavy gun emplacements were likewise being repaired behind the French coast.

It was no surprise therefore when on Friday, 6th September, Headquarters, Home Forces, issued the warning: "Attack probable within the next three days", and General Brooks, the commander, met with his Chiefs of Staff to decide if "Alert No. 1" (that is, the one which announced that invasion was imminent) should be issued, but it was agreed that the defence forces should stand by at immediate notice.

The same day special instructions were issued by Keith Park regarding the question of factory defence, for within his area lay the greater part of the key fighter production at that time. Consequently he ordered that special defence should be given not only to the obvious factories at Southampton where Spitfire production was concentrated, and to Hawker's at Kingston-on-Thames, but also to Brooklands and Langley. Twenty-four hours later the wisdom of this was brought forcibly home, for the factory at Brooklands where Hawker Hurricanes were produced was singled out as part of a policy of attacking fighter production centres that had just been introduced as an aid to the programme of attacking the fields of operational fighter squadrons.

That the situation was made graver by this was very clear but there followed one of those unexpected turns of events that helped to ease the situation since, instead of a continuance of these forms of attack, 7th September was suddenly marked by a switch to bombing the centre of London. Newspapers that were coming off the presses that morning may have offered some consolation to the workers from the capital who waited in their shelters—for these Luftwaffe raids were being delivered in daylight—as they carried such headlines as "RAF Fire Oil Tanks on Danube" before going on to describe raids on oil refineries at Regensburg on the Czechoslovakian frontier. However, the mood of the time was still concerned with invasion as the press announcement of two days later was to show with the words that demonstrated Bomber Command's concern at the build-up at Ostend: "We Check Threat of Invasion". Yet on the previous Saturday night the sounding of church bells, giving warning of parachutists being dropped, had been widespread.

It was the day before this false alarm that Göring had stood on the cliffs opposite 11 Group's chalk-walled coastline and watched three hundred bombers accompanied by twice as many fighters pass overhead. These with others were to drop in excess of 600 tons of bombs, so that at 8 p.m. that evening Eastern and Southern Commands were passed the codeword "Cromwell", indicating an imminent threat.

Forty-one of the bombers had later fallen to British guns together with a proportion of the fighters and it was the fall of one of these that provided a curious incident for a Mr and Mrs Whitmore. Coming down the street they were surprised to see the six-foot-tall figure of a young man of about twenty or so years of age. He was wearing a uniform they did not know but with it only one boot. Curious, they invited him in and were told in good English, "I am a German officer, I have had the misfortune to be brought down."

While Mr Whitmore telephoned the police his wife brought the German some sliced bread and butter which he washed down with two cups of tea, all the time playing with their small son, who showed him a toy aeroplane. Soon a knock came to the front door at the same time that the unexpected visitor was explaining his command of English by the fact that he had lived for two years in Manchester. The German rose to go, shaking hands all round before being conducted to the waiting police car. "Just my luck," was his final comment. "My wedding was to be next week."

Just how determined were the attacks at this time to wear away the strength and spirit of 11 Group is shown by a diary reference to the evening bombing that caused the civilian Alert to be sounded south of the Thames at 8.15 p.m. and not cancelled until 5.20 the following morning. This was in fact the first raid of what was to be the most sustained air attack to last for fifty-seven consecutive nights on London, since what is regarded as the final sorties were not flown until 2nd November, and a curious item of information to come out of the raids was that the Luftwaffe was reported to be using new bombs with concrete casings.

However, this new tactic was to bring relief to the much-punished fighter fields of 11 Group just as it was most welcome, and at such aerodromes as Hawkinge, where pilots were reported as having been lifted from their cockpits in a coma-like sleep, and Croydon, there was suddenly time to laze in the sun and to relax. The same was true of the afternoon, with empty skies until at about 4.30 p.m. the peace was suddenly shattered for No. 72 Squadron by the Tannoy crackling into life and ordering the Spitfires to be scrambled.

Seven machines hurtled into the air led by Flying Officer Elsdon, behind whom was Pilot Officer Douthwaite, who only six days before had scored his first victory over a Messerschmitt 109. The odds were enormous when they found the bombers, for of these there were 150 in tight-packed, text-book formation almost as if they were taking part in a flypast, but within a few minutes an accurately shooting gunner in a Messerschmitt 110 had accounted for the flight leader of the Spitfires, who had to bale out over the Thames Estuary severely wounded, while almost simultaneously Sergeant White was brought down in like manner.

With two aircraft lost and one now unserviceable there remained only four to answer the next call at 5.55 p.m., this time led by Flying Officer Holland, when the "Bandits" turned out to be a horde of sixty bombers heading for London with a fighter escort.

Landing again, the pilots were anxious to be released at 8 p.m., but even this was fifteen minutes late and their unease was heightened by the peculiar glow in the sky over London, which lay twelve miles off. Had they but known, it could be made out from Kenley, the Sector station even more distant, where it was seen as a great red light illuminating the whole of the northern horizon and which was to remain there waxing and waning like a breathing, live thing until it was swamped by daylight the following day. But for two of the No. 72 Squadron pilots there was to be no meal that evening, not even the touring Naafi van to supplement the serviceman's standby of "tea and wads", for the pair were ordered into the air again before reaching the Mess.

From 12,000 feet, Douthwaite and his colleage could see the cause, for the great glow that had so troubled them on the ground was a vast conflagration where the Thames turns north from Putney Bridge and even the water seemed to bubble and burn as thousands of tons of sugar floating on the water took fire.

The patrol line for the two machines was between Croydon and the Docks but the vigil was rewarded by only a sight of one raider as the gushes of light from the burning gasholders below sent up leaping reflections into the sky. With a quick reflex action as his thumb slammed down on the firing button, Douthwaite put in a burst of fire at 700 yards' range, but the distance was too great and the raider was merely warned of the presence of the Spitfires and became lost in the emptiness of the late summer night sky.

When the patrol was over a new problem beset the two

pilots, for it appeared that they would have to attempt the near-impossible and land at the Controller's bidding in an airfield surrounded by dwellings and with enemy bombers in the vicinity. The position was further complicated by the unavailability of both the duty pilot and the station commander. Clearly something had to be done and quickly, so that it was a sergeant who, after a search through the blacked-out control tower for the master switch, took responsibility for lighting up the aerodrome so that the two could land.

With their fuel gauges almost at zero the two Spitfires were taxied in and their pilots made weary tracks towards supper and a beer while away to the north the searchlights probed the sky that was the colour of flame.

But if the Battle of Britain was gradually becoming the Blitz, the change was taking place very slowly, so slowly in fact that no one realized at the time that the alteration of the Luftwaffe's tactics was something of an admission of defeat, for the daylight battle was to continue with little change. Yet the historic 7th September had its full crop of stories grave and gay, such as the mystery, still unexplained, of Sergeant Ronkal of No. 310 (Czech) Squadron. In fact this unit was based at Duxford, where the Sergeant had been sent to gain experience of Hawker Hurricanes. He was supposed to have carried out no more than a couple of familiarization flights, yet why did he stray into 11 Group's area and how did his gun button become set to "fire" when the wreckage of the abandoned machine was discovered thirty-two years later?

The strain of battle was now beginning to sap the strength of the flyers on both sides, not least the aircrews of the Luftwaffe, some of whom made two trips to the prime target that night. It was the same with the defenders, and especially those acting as Flight commanders such as Flight Lieutenant H. R. A. "Blue Blood" Beresford, in charge of No. 257 Squadron's "A" Flight at Martlesham Heath. He it was who before death had claimed him that early

September day made near-superhuman efforts to hold the
spirit of the squadron together before the arrival of Robert
Stanford Tuck in October. Beresford, plunged into gloom
by the situation and deeply worried by the trend of events,
would occasionally show the state of his nerves in private
by small but telling characteristics that developed, such as a
morbid preoccupation with the passage of time. As he sat
with a friend after a day in the air, he would constantly ask,
"Do you think there'll be a Blitz tomorrow?"

Almost as soon as the light grew sufficiently strong, with
that accompanying slight chill in the morning that gives the
first hint that summer has passed its peak, a lone Hurricane
was noted by some droning over the severely mauled
capital of England. The figure at the controls was a thin-
faced man, his features framed by a white flying helmet: Air
Vice-Marshal Park was, in the manner of his King, taking a
look for himself at the situation. Whatever the cost was
likely to be to the city, the change in tactics was in a manner
of speaking something of a deliverance, for from this point
forward the Battle of Britain could be fought to a conclusion
now that the unceasing punishment of the all-important
fighter stations seemed to be over. This fact seemed to be
endorsed by the relative quiet of the daylight hours,
although before 8 o'clock the following evening the sirens
were again wailing over a battered London where, twenty-
four hours before, men had spent the hours of darkness
manning their defence positions in the belief that the
bombing in fact heralded the long-awaited invasion.

There was something almost akin to the spirit of Drake
now, for there was ordered no emergency meeting of the
War Cabinet and no sign of panic, just a greater dependence
on what facilities for shelter existed although platforms of
the Underground system did not come into use until later.
Some areas were better off than others in what could be
offered in this direction and envious eyes were cast at
Ramsgate in Kent where, since they had been prepared by
the Borough Engineer and Surveyor in 1938, there existed

four miles of tunnels capable of giving cover to 60,000 people, half of them seated, at an initial cost that had worked out at exactly one pound per head to the ratepayers.

On the Monday following what one person recalls as a weekend in hell, when the shrapnel as people loosely called shell splinters had clattered down on the roofs of houses like steel rain, the pattern of the former raids seemed to be resumed in the afternoon. There were attacks on areas where aircraft factories were and savage aerial fights once more ensued, yet some pilots were to return to their bases and report that there was no sign of Nazi bombers, although the crews of these believed that it was possible to detect a new spirit in the audacity of the defence.

In part this may have been true, for Keith Park was not only employing fresh tactics of sending up paired squadrons of defending fighters: some new blood had been injected into 11 Group by the change of units which had taken place over the previous few days. These moves were not always popular, as when for instance No. 111 Squadron had been sent to Drem and No. 43 Squadron had departed from the battered Tangmere. A further contribution to the new spirit was, apart from the withdrawal of wearied units, the ending of the policy that kept 11 Group's squadrons at Readiness throughout the daylight hours. The result was that units such as No. 92 Squadron, newly drafted to the group, were worn down less quickly than those before, and an attempt on the part of the Luftwaffe to repeat the surprise of 7th September found 11 Group ready. The force of one hundred bombers that was intercepted over Dover in splendid weather was severely dealt with, so that the confidence of those which succeeded in reaching London where the City and West End were bombed suffered in proportion; perhaps it was this which prompted Admiral Raeder to report on the following day, "There is no sign of the defeat of the enemy's air force over southern England and in the Channel area."

The following day it seemed that events were about to

come to a head when Dover suffered a severe attack from the air and a simultaneous bombardment from the cross-Channel guns. At the same time there had been something of a heartening reciprocal action, for the Admiralty had announced a few hours before that a "strong and repeated offensive action" by British light naval forces against shipping concentrations and ports, "which would be vital to the enemy in the event of an attempt to invade England".

The day had another piece of heartening news as well, for Buckingham Palace had been bombed, destroying a private chapel, and this, one of several occasions when the home of the royal family was to be damaged, made civilian and serviceman alike feel that all were equally "in it together".

Even so, the threat of invasion ran through men's thoughts like a flashing beacon of imminent danger so that no one was surprised when Winston Churchill stated in a broadcast that the Nazis were preparing for invasion even at that moment, and that troops were ready and ships massing from Hamburg to Brest. Certainly Sir Dudley Pound had only hours before informed the War Cabinet of the "fair numbers" of vessels still entering Boulogne, Calais, Flushing and Ostend, a concentration which totalled according to unofficial sources 1,700 craft, a figure that some said was to rise to 2,500.

The weather had deteriorated about now. Haze and an overcast sky with occasional showers were the order of the day. Even so there was plenty of activity in the group due to enemy action, although that near to the heart as mid-month approached was mainly confined to ceaseless attacks by single enemy aircraft during the day. There was more concentration during the nights, which were punctuated by tremendous barrages of anti-aircraft fire with an average of one hundred rounds per gun being fired. This was regarded as an essential part of the defence since it was reported that on the night of 12th September, for instance, the first raiders that had been reported between 12 and 16,000 feet were replaced by later arrivals at some 27,000 feet, flying 60 m.p.h. faster.

September 13th was a Friday, but in spite of the feelings of the over-superstitious in official circles, the omens were regarded as promising. It was now that the Ministry of Health decided that public morale was improving, a fact that was regarded as detrimental to the hopes of a renewed evacuation scheme for civilians. It was when the War Cabinet was discussing this point and adding that a new threat existed in the fact that sewer pipes had been put out of action by the bombing, that a familiar sound could be heard above. It had the note that all had now come to associate with the unsynchronized motors of an enemy, and before many minutes had passed its hostile intentions were made clear, for the machine loosed the first of a stick of half a dozen bombs. In fact although the raider was seen to be low and unchallenged over Downing Street, it was Buckingham Palace that again suffered, King George VI and Queen Elizabeth having just returned from Windsor at that moment, so they were not more than eighty yards from the explosions although none of the royal family sustained injury. It was this type of thing that typified Nazi activity over the Group at this period in addition to reconnaissance flights, and in the main these audacious sorties were successful due to the difficulties in hunting them that the indifferent weather now presented, although the hours of darkness which followed found some 150 bombers over central London.

It appeared now that No. 11 Group's struggle was past its peak, a fact that was quietly remarked upon by the better informed of Park's Operations Room staff. However, the problem still remained of accurately judging the mood of the enemy and what form future attacks would take, a task that appeared to be impossible, for apart from the certainty of a break in the weather wrought by the changing seasons there was nothing to guide such a forecast.

CHAPTER ELEVEN

The Thames Afire

Today, with questionable accuracy, we celebrate Sunday 15th September as Battle of Britain Day but the reason for the weight of daylight attacks that materialized within that period of twenty-four hours is not difficult to find since they were born out of the conference of the previous day, during which Hitler examined the situation then existing. Perhaps now those who sat round the table with him in Berlin noticed a certain indecision over whether to call off the invasion attempt or to let matters proceed, for this was the first time in the European struggle that Nazi Germany had suffered anything even approaching a defeat and it had been inflicted by an enemy that had seemingly been vanquished three or four months before with an air force of which intelligence reports had been contemptuous.

The key to the decision that must be made was obviously the likely outcome of the bombing attacks and it was clear that these should be allowed to continue if an invasion was to be contemplated. "The enemy recovers again and again," the Führer complained only to be assured by Göring that in the end the Luftwaffe would triumph, so that it was finally decided that a further three days would be granted to achieve this aim.

With the operations date so close it was essential that a renewal of effort be made immediately, particularly as the future climatic conditions were not likely to favour either flying on the scale demanded or a Channel crossing of the required strength for much longer, and since the forecast for the fateful Sunday was extremely favourable the preparations began at once.

The day began much as had many of the earlier ones with the inevitable reconnaissance patrols by the Luftwaffe over 11 Group's area. Much of the preceding months' fighting had spilled over these borders into the adjacent groups, particularly into that of Air Chief Marshal Leigh-Mallory, who commanded the area to the north. From here the co-operation had not always been cordial or complete. The same was not true of overlapping responsibilities to the west, where Air Vice-Marshal Brand had always given help immediately, and the sensitive bordering targets at Southampton and Portsmouth meant that this was not infrequently called for.

However that may have been the coming day was to be largely an 11 Group affair and the first hostile tracks did not appear on the plotting tables until shortly after 11 a.m., the RDF stations having picked them up shortly before. It was obvious that this was the big attack which might also be the last throw and eleven squadrons were scrambled to intercept from 11 Group alone. The weather was largely cloudless except over the Straits where there were intermittent showers and over London where eighty per cent of the sky was clouded over. The weather was less pleasant in these parts and the first nips of autumn could be discerned. One pilot noted that he borrowed a pair of fleece-lined trousers

Barrage balloons were frequently the target for Messerschmitts ahead of bomber formations, particularly over towns on the south-east coast as here

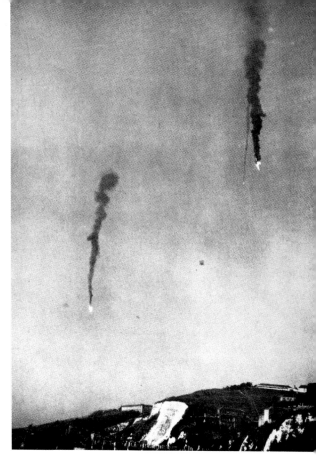

An attack at very low level was carried out on Folkestone at midday on 26th August

Where the Queen's Gallery now stands was once a private chapel hit by bombs from a raider on 13th September, with these results. Buckingham Palace had also been bombed three days before this incident

As day and night raiding overlapped, 11 Group had a double responsibility. On the night of 27th September fires were started in London's Chancery Lane among other places. The following morning firemen were still at work

Sergeant pilot H. R. N. Mitchell, a New Zealander, poses in front of Hawker Hurricane "J" of No. 615 Squadron at Northolt in October 1940

Left to right facing camera, Josef Schmidt, Ernst Udet and Hermann Göring discuss plans; the first is said to have grossly underestimated British strength before the battle

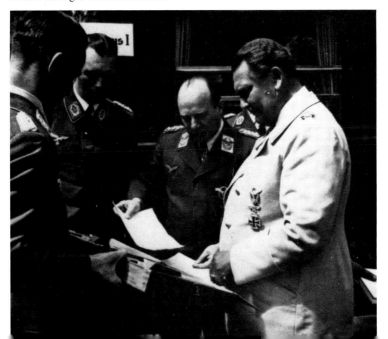

A Heinkel 111 of KG100 is prepared for another trip by the ground crew at Vannes, France

A stack of 500 kg. SC (Sprengbombe Cylindrisch), thin-wall, general purpose, high-explosive bombs await loading into the vertical racks of the Heinkel 111s in the background; that nearest the camera has a protective cover over the nose perspex

Above left: With the corrugated skin of a Junkers 52/3m as a background, Hitler acknowledges greetings from a reception party

Above right: Bomb-aimer of a Junkers Ju 88A-1 checks his instrument before a sortie by a Staffel 2 aircraft

Below: Hitler, with Hermann Göring who turns his back to the camera, congratulates Nazi Luftwaffe officers during 1940

Nazi airmen relax while their Messerschmitt 109Es are prepared in the background. All use deckchairs, except the man in the centre who has a relegated aircraft seat

Offset forward gondola of a Junkers 88, showing the rear hatch open and swung down. Bombs on the external racks are SC500s

A Junkers Ju88 over the Thames Estuary photographed from the rear of the forward gondola on a similar machine. The MG81 gun fills the foreground

With the insignia of the Geschwader 1A on its side, the Messerschmitt 109E-3 flown by Major Schellmann awaits repair to its combat damage sustained in 1940. Extension of the top surface camouflage over the normally light blue sides shows one of several variations that could be introduced at Staffel level

A Luftwaffe pilot who had been rescued from the sea poses with his Royal Engineer captors. He was reported at the time to be named Werner Voight who had flown a Messerschmitt 109. It is now believed he is Oberleutnant Vogt of 4/JG3, shot down off Abbots Cliff on 11th October

A captured Luftwaffe NCO wearing forage cap and flight blouse is brought ashore on a stretcher by an ARP worker from a First Aid Party in front, and a member of the Red Cross. The civilian may be a doctor, and a postman brings up the rear

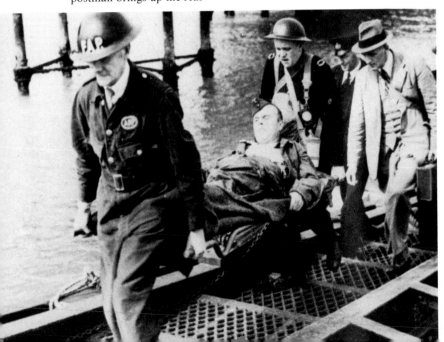

for his patrol, which allowed him to fly with an open hood that enabled him to see much better.

Meanwhile, mindful that history was about to be made, Churchill, with an almost uncanny judgement of the situation, made another of his visits to 11 Group Headquarters, arriving a little less than thirty minutes before the first tracks were reported in the underground room.

With the usual fearful odds largely continuing to prevail the interceptors pitched into the first Dorniers with guns blazing, although some squadrons were to report finding no enemy to engage: No. 152, scrambled twice that day with negative results, was an example. Those that could join battle found the mixture as it had been for some time now, although the Nazi crews were to note later in their reports that they found their reception more spirited than it had been for some time past, no doubt this being attributable to the introduction of fresh pilots to the main British fighting zone. Some of these were noting changes themselves at this time for several reports speak of enemy machines returning fire with defence weapons with a slower rate of fire than the machine guns usually employed, a fact that would seem to indicate that the defensive cannon usually associated with the autumn months of 1940 were in fact already coming into use.

Nazi fighters were now less in evidence and it was possible for the defenders to concentrate on the bombers without the harassment of attacks by their equals. One pilot reported that after he had been unable to send down a Dornier immediately, eight of his colleagues set on the machine and made certain of the kill, although circumstances such as this were rare.

It was early afternoon when the second wave of the main attack was spotted and for this many of the pilots who had been up for the first reception committee had recently returned by unusual routes. Reports speak of several who had been downed by the raiders not too far from their home bases returning by public transport so that a tram conductor still remembers his astonishment on coming down the stairs to collect the fares on the lower deck at finding a young man in flying kit and with a rolled-up parachute under his arm holding up a few coins and asking for "A threepenny one, please". In fact the conductor allowed him to travel free (against company regulations).

The conditions of the day were so confused that the Luftwaffe crews found accurate bombing was impossible, with the result that bombs were scattered not only over London but also over the residential districts south of the Thames.

Yet, quite apart from the main attacks that were made on London, the Nazis also did not fail to attempt the destruction of other important targets, so that at about mid-afternoon a force was sent off to bomb Portland. The same was true of similar areas in 11 Group and thus it was that the Erprobungsgruppe 210, now flying under the command of its second new leader, was sent to bomb the Spitfire shops of Supermarine's Woolston works. They were met by a tremendous barrage of anti-aircraft fire. During the approach to the target they had enjoyed the advantage of cloud cover, for the day had now sharply deteriorated, but there still existed the problems posed by the barrage balloons. These, in the event, the formation avoided with ease and dived in to their bombing run with no fighter opposition so far encountered. However, for some reason (some suggest that it was due to the very fierce and accurate ground fire), none of the bombs dropped did any damage to the factory. This was to come rather later and with some thoroughness.

The attacking Messerschmitt 110s were rid of their loads and heading out across the Solent for home when retribution arrived in the shape of the Hurricane squadron, long resident at Tangmere, No. 607, which swept into the hostile formation as it was passing over the Isle of Wight in the vicinity of the Needles, suffering no losses but claiming no kills.

Thus ended the day when the RAF had been forced to meet the full onslaught of the Nazi Luftwaffe brought to its operational zenith. There were other attacks delivered throughout the historic twenty-four hours and a break-down of the units which were employed also gives a typical example of the raids after lunchtime that were delivered in the London area alone. The first of these were over the target at about ten minutes before one o'clock and consisted of more than twenty aircraft of LG2 carrying high-explosive and oil bombs. It was not until almost 1 p.m. that the next bombers appeared in about equal number, Dornier 17zs of III/KG76 from their base at Cormeilles-en-Vexin. The Lille-based Heinkel 111s of II/KG53 arrived some two and a half hours later with similar loads but with the exception of the oil bombs. Incendiaries and high explosive formed the mixed loads of KG3's Dornier 17zs that were overhead at almost the same time, the unit putting into the air almost every aircraft on charge. The loads continued to be mixed from the twenty-seven Heinkels flying from Gilze-Rijen which were next reported fifteen minutes later and the same is true of the remaining bombers, all overhead within a maximum of eight minutes, these being the Dornier 17zs once more, this time from their bases at Saint-Leger (II/ KG2) and Cambrai (III/KG2).

At the end of the day came the time to count the costs and both the RAF and the Luftwaffe claimed that the day had been a success. Of these claims the British one was perhaps the less easily proved, if only due to the fact that a high proportion of the enemy machines brought down had been lost over the sea and consequently were not subject to final confirmation. However, it is certain that the enemy did not expect such severe losses as were sustained and it must have called for an enormous conceit not to realize that the opposition in the form of No. 11 Group had won the victory. Even so, Keith Park thought that something even better could have been achieved and thus it was that he listed a number of errors committed that day and advised changes in tactics which would prevent a repetition of the situation. That this was possible on the next day was due to a sharp deterioration in the weather, for there was now a low cloud base and persistent rain that successfully prevented air activity on any scale.

The lessons that Park felt had been learned during the previous day included one that indicated an undue time-lag by the Group's controllers in vectoring the new paired squadrons on to raids, perhaps due to unfamiliarity with the new system and the allied practice of sending single squadrons to large raids. In addition to this Park noted that the paired units were also tending to rendezvous too low and too far forward, with the large massed groups of the enemy receiving special attention, although this was often where the escorting fighters were found, with the result that the bombers at lower altitude escaped unchallenged.

These were not all of Park's criticisms. Others covered what he considered to be plain errors, but as will be seen most of the faults were concerned with the new system and the remedies were comparatively simple. These included an order that in future the smaller raids were to be intercepted by fighters operating on patrol lines kept short, and in case it was merely a lack of information that gave an inadequate picture of the raid strength these patrols should be made up of four squadrons, two at altitude and a further pair somewhere above 15,000 feet, Spitfires being sent to deal with the enemy high-flyers.

Meanwhile the Hurricane squadrons were to be assembled at the fighter aerodromes nearer to the Sector stations, although those from Tangmere and Northolt were to operate as three wings after being held in reserve until the later waves appeared, for it was these that normally contained the bombers, the fighters usually forming the advance guard.

As one might expect, the classic day had its fair share of legend that began to accumulate almost at once, but one of the strangest is the positive identification of a Junkers 90, a four-engined transport that is claimed to have been seen at such a low altitude over Croydon in Surrey that its national markings could be made out with, on its tail, a pair of attacking Spitfires.

Yet despite the size of the operations on what was later to be called the "Greatest Day" the onslaughts continued, although now they had to become less frequent due to the weather. By now this was showing the first signs of beginning a series of problems, for the Battle of Britain weather that most alive at the time recall was about to fade. The two days after the busy Sunday were punctuated by squally showers, although Tuesday, 17th September, saw some raids attempted over 11 Group, raids that had to be kept small as the forecast indicated no clearance that would permit mass attacks. The individual formations that crossed the coast in the Deal and Dover sector comprised only about forty machines each, "Hell's Corner" however on this occasion escaping the bomb and shell attacks of the previous day.

Inevitably, Hitler personally asked for reports on the huge raid that Göring had promised would be the first to bring the RAF to its knees, and at the same time he was to demand an analysis of the effect that the work of the British Bomber Command had on the great fleet of invasion vessels that had been built up. To this the Naval Staff in Berlin saw fit to add a comment, and its concluding words were to help the Nazi leader make up his mind more than anything else. They ran: "The enemy air force is by no means defeated." There was nothing for it now but to postpone "Operation Sealion", the intended invasion of the island fortress, although the announcement was at pains to point out that this was not a cancellation.

Thus it was that the main operation against Great Britain was to take place after the fall of darkness that day. This fact in itself indicated a victory for the RAF, since the types of operation that were now to become the pattern of events were totally different both in intent and execution from the daylight raiding, although the emergence of them posed a whole new set of problems with the introduction of night fighting that went beyond the limits of the Battle of Britain. Emphasis was now largely on London and here the bombs of this night fell over a wide area, damaging Burlington Arcade, Berkeley Square, Bond Street, Park Lane and Whitehall itself, although twenty people died while under cover in the subway at Marble Arch. This was, in the manner of the day, lined with white tiles and these, torn away and shattered into splinters by the blast of a bomb, became deadly sharp projectiles.

The following night saw an intensification of the new attacks so that the John Lewis store in Oxford Street was reduced to a jumble of masonry between the stark walls. Not far away at the famous Circus, the front of Peter Robinson's store was smashed in by bombing although the building remained standing. Elsewhere the headquarters of the London County Council at County Hall was hit and the famous library of the Inner Temple also suffered. This was the eleventh successive raid that the capital had endured and people were beginning to look for a means of protection during what now promised to be a long-drawn-out campaign. There was supposed to be no taking refuge in the tunnels of the Underground system as had taken place during the previous conflict, twenty-two years before, but by now people were openly buying platform tickets for one and a half (old) pence to get a night's sleep and companionship. Of this, Churchill openly expressed his approval but some Cabinet ministers were not of his opinion.

Even so, despite the obvious change of policy by the enemy, the bright weather that was now replacing the poorer conditions of earlier days meant that 11 Group still had to fight a daylight battle a little later than had been the practice in high summer, in fact from around 9 a.m. when the first raiders began to be picked out on the cathode-ray tubes that kept electronic watch on the other side of the Channel. The raiders when they appeared were in the main not bombers but fighters, which crossed the coast between Dover and Folkestone at some 20,000 feet. To counter this threat a number of squadrons were scrambled by 11 Group, including No. 249 that had moved into North Weald on 1st September to relieve No. 56 Squadron whose machines and ground staff they took over. It was the first of four alerts that they were to answer that day and the weather had reverted to its earlier form sufficiently for the pilots to lounge out of doors in deckchairs between each sortie to wait for the next order that never failed to cause stomach-tightening muscle spasms.

Over Maidstone the raiders were broken up and what bombers there were singled out for particular attention by another squadron before a return to base to await the next call. It was not long in coming, the pilots racing to their machines at North Weald just as the hands of the clocks with their bright colour-change triangles in the Operations Rooms pointed to 11 a.m. No. 249 was paired with No. 46 Squadron on this occasion to intercept a raid of more than sixty "bandits". The bombers this time were Heinkel 111s which had the advantage of great towering clouds of cumulus to provide cover, operating with an escort of Me 109s. One combat report speaks of a pilot's first sight of a group from this raid, consisting of about twenty bombers whose presence was shown to the British pilots by the bursts of anti-aircraft shells. As the two units swept in, the Messerschmitts were seen to be manoeuvring to take on the interceptors so that there was no time for more than a swift exchange of fire before action had to be broken off due to the risk of collision at the tremendous closing speed of the opposing fighters. The Heinkels are reported to have jettisoned their bombs at this stage and set course for base without the fighter protection so that, after inflicting some small damage the two squadrons returned to base.

Off the ground for the third time on that Wednesday, the interceptors from the same paired squadrons failed to find any of the raiders, although what they did see was an awe-inspiring sight. Below them the oil storage tanks at the mouth of the Thames Estuary were ablaze. Great billowing clouds of black smoke were churning over in rolling masses as the wind pulled them out into a top-heavy mass and the flames below were of such an intensity as they leapt up contrasting sharply with their dark background that the reflection in the water, even during daylight, seemed to give the impression that the Thames also was ablaze.

On the fourth scramble the ominous clouds were still there, now reaching 8,000 feet into the air, and so were ten or more Heinkel 111s. One of the pilots who judged that on this occasion there was no escort threw his machine into a screaming dive straight at one of the leading bombers. At a range of less than fifty yards he pressed the gun button and at the same instant the enemy pilot saw what was coming. Through the large glazed nose that housed part of the crew it was possible to see the German's reaction as he swung the controls to bank away from the danger. In this he failed and the fire blasted into the bomber's front. With pieces falling away and trailing a half-opened parachute the bomber made an almost leisurely turnover and then with sickening speed roared down almost vertically into the estuary of the Thames. Squadron 249 returned to base to find a pair of congratulatory telegrams awaiting them thanking the pilots for their achievement three days earlier. They were from the Chief of Air Staff, Cyril Newall, and Archibald Sinclair, the Secretary of State for Air.

Although actions such as this were typical of the day's activities there were many squadrons engaged for this brief renewal of the former state of affairs, since the pilot shortage had in part been remedied by the agreement of further increased allocations of men for the coming four-week period, and also the squadrons flying the Merlin-engined Fairey Battle were to have some of their pilots taken and trained in single-seat techniques to make good the average of some twenty or so pilots which each squadron of fighters lacked according to figures supplied at the beginning of the month.

As September advanced the activities of the Luftwaffe over 11 Group's area slowly became less and the primary target for the daylight raiders on the following Thursday was once again the tanks at the Thames Estuary despite the poorer weather. Then, by some strange mischance, the following day seemed to present an event which took the Group completely by surprise. There had been the usual early morning sorties mounted mainly by reconnaissance machines and little else was really anticipated by the defences since although the weather was by this day clearer with some bright periods, there were persistent squalls of rain. Locally, however, conditions were very good. It was about 10.30 a.m. when the blips on the RDF screens suddenly began to show a build-up of enemy forces over the French coast—a strange factor of the whole summer being that the Luftwaffe was in the habit of building up its massed formations in full view of 11 Group's surveillance—and now it was evident that something unexpected was afoot.

Just how unexpected matters were is shown by the fact that many of the British fighter squadrons were at the low state of preparedness termed "thirty minutes available", so that the pilots and ground crews expected the intermediate "readiness". Not so on this occasion, however, for greatly to their surprise several squadrons were scrambled from the low state. The attack they were expected to intercept was about to be delivered in two waves of some sixty Messerschmitt single-seaters in total and at about 13,000 feet or so the formation crossed the British coast in the vicinity of Dungeness, making it clear that towns on the River Medway were the likely target. Four squadrons from Hornchurch and Biggin Hill made the interception over Maidstone and a fierce fight ensued, made the more savage when the later arrivals were set upon by the second Nazi wave. A running fight developed during the retreat of the enemy but this was a case of fighter against fighter, very different from the earlier cases when the Messerschmitts had been forced to keep their activities to a minimum in order to protect bombers. The result was a rather salutary lesson for the Group since several Hurricanes and Spitfires were lost, either damaged or destroyed.

The following day was Saturday, 21st September, and it was the date on which it became clear that the type of activity of the previous day was to become the new norm, for it was marked by a set of intrusions similar to those of the previous day. This time the greater number of British squadrons was scrambled in the early evening and although the bulk of the daylight hours found London enjoying relative quiet, this was the target of the Messerschmitt sweeps that no less than twenty No. 11 Group squadrons were sent to engage, although in the event only one of them was successful.

This new pattern seemed to be about to be repeated over the area after a comparative lapse on the following Monday. Once again the massing of enemy formations was witnessed over the Calais area. This time the readings indicated a large force of aircraft, which turned out to be Messerschmitts once more acting in an independent role. The use of what had always been regarded as fighters in this offensive manner was something comparatively new, and in some semi-official quarters it was seen as an indication of a Luftwaffe bomber shortage. This was reflected in the press reports at the time, which spoke of the single-seaters making "one dive attack at 400 miles an hour . . . and then they tried to escape". In fact what witnesses were seeing was the pioneer use of the modern fighter-bomber and not an enemy suffering from a bomber shortage. About half of the interceptor squadrons sent up by 11 Group managed to find the enemy that made up the initial wave. It was the third attack of similar nature that day that one witness was able to watch as it ran into a patrol of Spitfires not far from Hythe. "Two of the enemy had just peeled off from the group of Messerschmitts very high up and out over the sea when Spitfires closed in to attack. One of these spotted the movement and detached himself from his squadron and went screeching down behind at full cock. For a split second I had a vision of three roaring planes flashing across the sky." The witness then went on to tell how the first of the enemy single-seaters seemed intent on shooting up a target on the ground in ignorance of the fate of his fellow further aft. Meanwhile this machine was receiving the full weight of the fire-power of the Spitfire's eight Brownings, and pieces would seem to have begun breaking off as smoke started to stream from the enemy.

But if this was to be the future pattern of daylight raiding as the month advanced it also became clear that the night raider was part of the new order of things. It evolved that British bombers were passing one way across the coast at much the same time as Nazi machines were crossing in the opposite direction, London all the while being the target for the latter. This was probably the reason for the final sanction of the use of the stations of the capital's Underground railway at last for shelterers, Aldwych being the first to be pressed into use with a suddenness that surprised even Churchill in view of the attitudes struck previously by the Home Secretary and the Minister of Transport, who did not bother even to inform the Prime Minister of the decision. Aldwych was chosen no doubt due to its being a terminus and thus having no Piccadilly Line through-traffic.

CHAPTER TWELVE

Autumn Leaves

With the last days of September almost in sight and with them the first suggestion of the end of the fine summer, it seemed that a change too was about to take place in the course of the air war for No. 11 Group. There were certainly those that claimed later that the new horror of the fire raids, which were to come as the leaves turned brown and dropped from the trees were a greater trial than the ordeal by high explosive that had marked the high days of summer.

Statisticians claim that the Battle of Britain lasted for 114 days, although the exact justification for this seems difficult as the beginning, like the end, was not clear-cut. Nor was the transition into the various phases that were once much discussed. Strangely, although the period was not one calculated to give the impression that the enemy was in any way beaten, outside the fighting area the demands of service life certainly occupied the minds of airmen far more than the events of the larger world, and the prolific diary-keeper "Sammy" Samson could summon up no more for his daily record than that Prestwick was "still very quiet . . . as regards enemy activity, but bags of training flying". However, ten days later the rumours of a move south were substantiated when the squadron at 7.20 p.m. on 8th October began the shift to Northolt, where the inevitable sorting of kit followed the arrival, "tired and worn out", at 2.50 p.m. the following day.

Similarly, the battle that was still being waged had but little effect on the life of Sergeant pilot Peter Ward-Smith, at that time with the Flying Training School at Little Rissington in the Cotswolds. Here everyone seemed completely out of touch with reality, with the result that very few took seriously anything that was written in the newspapers or broadcast on the wireless. The result was that their whole life was taken up with flying, playing darts in the Mess, more flying, drinking scrumpy in the local, then more flying, and so on until the course was completed. The background of danger at home or depressing news meant absolutely nothing and the only slim connection with reality was the occasional overheard remark from the instructors as to what they would do if the quiet little haven of the aerodrome was suddenly violated by the appearance of Nazi bombers. In this, although all the staff had a frequently voiced desire to "sort the bastards out", there was little chance of an opportunity as they were never allowed to join an operational squadron. The best defensive manoeuvre they seemed able to devise, restricted as they were to flying unarmed training machines, was to agree to circle the base, although it was never made clear in what manner this was supposed to frustrate the attackers— Ward-Smith suggests it may have been to distract the bomb-aimers!

But occasionally the gravity of the situation centred largely in No. 11 Group did win through against such immediate problems as a complete absence of plugs in the baths on the station with the result that each man carried his personal one in the breast pocket of his tunic. The intrusion of the outer world might take place quite quickly and with some heat, when for instance a pupil was "carpeted" before the commanding officer perhaps after forgetting to lower the undercarriage of a Harvard trainer, when he would be made suddenly aware that to import this machine (they were the first American machines to be used by the RAF, having been ordered in June 1938 as part of the Expansion Scheme) other men's lives and valuable shipping had been put at risk to bring just one such trainer across the Atlantic.

A more personal realization of the situation in the world was awaiting the pair from Little Rissington who managed to get a 48-hour pass and made up their minds to make the journey to London by motor-cycle. They stopped at a pub somewhere in Wiltshire where a sing-song was going on in the bar. The two had scarcely entered the door when the chorus died away and a sudden quiet descended at the sight of their uniforms; in an amazed silence the two men walked towards the counter where each ordered a beer, their puzzlement changed to surprise when they turned to find that their order had been anticipated and some half-dozen pints were ready and waiting with freshly foaming heads on the top of the piano. The two young men had scarcely recovered their composure before a veritable storm of congratulations broke out and their hands were shaken until almost sore to the accompaniment of back-slapping, roars of "Good luck" from the assembly and remarks that the news told of 150 enemy machines having been brought down the previous day.

Thus it was that the two airmen understood the extreme gravity of the situation and how they represented symbols of the only protection that the country reckoned it had. Yet in fact airmen outside the fighting area had little desire to be more aware of what was going on beyond their own sphere and leaves were fully taken up with the problems of getting home and back again. If this meant a journey through London it could be a salutary experience, so it was inviting to draw about oneself again the cocoon of service life and occupy the mind with matters created by perhaps a conversion course to fighters which might take place at some backwater in Wales, there to become familiar with the intricacies of a Spitfire cockpit. From this one might look down on the crowded beaches at Rhyl, shoot at wrecks in the Dee or chase the elusive target of the towed drogue, so that gradually familiarity gained in close formation flying and other manoeuvres allowed the mind to take in the fact that here were no fierce monsters of the air as the first impressions were, but somewhat elderly machines with pump undercarts and constant-speed airscrews.

Yet despite diversions such as these there was in fact little reduction in air activity over No. 11 Group despite the shortening days of September, although it might be argued that the focal point had seemed to shift to the periphery of the group's area. For on its western boundary where it joined Brand's No. 10 Group and with which an amicable and seldom failing co-operation existed, there lay the important industrial centre of Southampton with Portsmouth nearby, both only a very short distance from Tangmere Sector Station and Westhampnett.

As the hands of the clock crept past 1.30 p.m. on the afternoon of Tuesday 24th September, the Radiolocation stations were doing their work well. The one so recently punished on the Isle of Wight, like its fellows with a range similar to its television counterpart of the day in the region of only forty miles, had picked up the echoes of a large Nazi formation at 15,000 feet and heading for Portsmouth. This was confirmed by the Observer Corps, which counted a total of seventeen raiders, so that a red alert was in operation although for some reason the public sirens had not sounded.

At much the same time, Fireman Ernest Dicker was on duty at Southampton Fire Station. Up to now his work had been comparatively routine with occasional relief wrought by such duties as standing by for a long day when trains of petrol wagons had been unloaded in an atmosphere of as much secrecy as could be managed with military police restricting the entrance of traffic to the immediate vicinity; soon all this was to change and the bells would go down in increasing number.

It was now a matter of seconds past the half-hour as Police Constable Williams of the Southampton Borough Police, not yet combined with the Hampshire Constabulary's 605-strong force—a war-time measure still three years off—was on his beat that took him past the boundary of Eastleigh aerodrome where the prototype Spitfire had made its maiden flight only four years earlier. Now the type was in full production at the Supermarine Company's works at Woolston and Itchen. The sound of aircraft engines was therefore not unusual but the note which met his ears on this occasion had something unfamiliar about it, so he scanned the clouds.

What in fact he was listening to was the sound of the thirty-four Daimler Benz liquid-cooled motors that powered the gaggle of Messerschmitt 110s that were even at that moment making landfall over Hamble after flying directly up Southampton Water, having turned from their original course. The formation which was drawn from Erprobungsgruppe 210, the same experimental group that had so punished Croydon aerodrome in the middle of the previous month, now began suddenly to peel off individually to make separate attacks on the Spitfire production shops on the waterfront itself. It required the scream and crash of the falling bombs to cause the civil warning to be given, but on this occasion the roar of the detonations was accompanied by the barking of the anti-aircraft guns and later one of the raiders was seen to be going down leaving a long zigzag of greasy black smoke over Portsmouth when a shell from the ground had burst directly above its nose.

But for the workers in the factory, many of whom were

still finishing their lunch, there was no time to observe such details as these, although the policeman, with his blue steel helmet pulled well down, took what cover he could find and wished that side-arms, in the use of which they had recently been trained as an additional invasion precaution, were permitted on the beat, if only to relieve his feelings. However, lacking the heavy old-fashioned weapons with which they had been temporarily issued, and which he personally felt were too heavy to enable the user to take proper aim at anything, he could now act only as an unwilling observer of the carnage that was to come.

The scramble to take cover was less calm than the later reports would have readers believe but on the other hand it was not in the nature of the Englishman of 1940 to stoop to panic. Of the two sets of works, that at Itchen was the better sited in relation to its shelters and a few workers from here managed to reach safety, but further along the road, Woolston was less lucky and some of the bombs which missed the factory here demolished a railway arch further along under which many were seeking what cover they could. It collapsed on top of them and the greater number of casualties resulted from this single incident.

Leaving the works only slightly damaged with light roofs blasted away and few if any of the windows intact, the raiding Messerschmitts then withdrew only to fly over Portsmouth in an arrogant manner such as Göring would have applauded; this was not a single pass but a series of flyovers, with first one machine and then another diving away from the main formation and then rejoining it. This tactic occupied a period of some twenty minutes, more than twice as long as the raid itself, and throughout the time there was no sign of the RAF, either from No. 11 or 10 Groups. The fact is that on this occasion the muddle of reporting the approach of the raiders had won for them a surprise victory and for once Park, the brilliant tactician, had been deceived so that the Nazis, unworried by dwindling fuel as they would have been further inland, particularly had single-seaters been used, had enjoyed a field-day over the Solent towns, only Leutnant von der Horst and Obergefreiter Ollers whose machine came down in the sea paying the supreme price.

The following day luck was again with the Luftwaffe, for flying above the cover afforded by broken cloud through which the sun peeped only intermittently came a single Dornier 17z. The barks of the guns in the distance were the first warning that anyone had of its approach and when almost over the Spitfire factory, the twin-engined machine suddenly appeared in a shallow dive and made a leisurely pass, so low that the markings were clearly visible on the side. Within the brave crew were toiling over the vertical camera that was recording every detail of their colleagues' work on the previous afternoon. Before anything could be done to intercept, the Dornier turned, climbed and was lost to sight heading towards the Isle of Wight over Southampton Water.

Outside the group's area, Bristol's Filton was bombed together with Plymouth, the poor dismembered remains of probably Unteroffiziers Hanft and Weidner from a 7/KG55 Heinkel 111 which was shot down after raiding the Bristol centre being collected by "the chap from the mortuary", remembers Sergeant Leigh of the Gloucesters, "appropriately in two dustbins". Inexplicably it was this night that saw the headcount of shelterers in the London Tube stations at its highest nightly total. Peter Ward-Smith recalls his feeling of nausea from the stench of human bodies stretched the length of the platforms all of which required to be carefully stepped over, although on the other side of the coin one woman summed matters up when she remarked, "It's marvellous to feel really safe for a few pence."

On 26th September the Polish Squadron at Northolt was honoured by a visit from King George VI. At the time of the inspection they were at readiness and the royal visit had to be curtailed when the Hurricanes were hastily scrambled to meet a raid in the Portsmouth vicinity. The King, left somewhat in suspense, asked for the results of the interception to be telephoned to him at Buckingham Palace. His Majesty might have been less pleased with matters had he known that his hosts were rapidly establishing a fighting reputation repugnant to the Western European mind, with the result that some of the new intake into the RAF from this source were somewhat far from the image that the news media of the day tried hard to present; Englishmen with unusual accents. Cases exist of enemy aircrew being machine-gunned by Polish pilots, and of their taking turns to blast a parachutist with their eight Brownings, but such sights were merely interpreted by those who saw the incidents as erroneous recognition of aircraft type and it was assumed that in each case the victim was British and the murderers Nazi. There is at least one case on record also of a foreign pilot at the controls of a Hawker Hurricane killing his hapless victim in a most horrific manner by means of deliberately milling him as he hung from the parachute straps, the subsequent damage to the airscrew making it necessary for a forced landing to be made by the Polish pilot.

Photographs of Southampton taken back by the reconnaissance Dornier of the previous day were quickly interpreted to reveal that the damage inflicted had been light, so the assault on this Thursday afternoon was intended to be in the nature of a knock-out blow. The weather in this corner of No. 11 Group was certainly on the side of the attackers for it presented a veritable wall of cumulus piled up over the Solent and stretching back over the northern shore of the Isle of Wight towards which came a massed formation of over seventy bombers with escorting fighters, the latter spread out over a five-mile spearhead that had assembled over Brittany. Not to be caught napping again the civilian sirens were sounded in plenty of time but they were scarcely necessary, for the sound of the motors' uneven beat was audible while the raiders were still well out to sea.

It was just about 5.35 p.m. when the advance guard made landfall on the Hampshire coast, their presence being made known by an attack on the balloon barrage. The individual balloons seemed suddenly to crumple up into a falling star of light leaving a long trail of dark grey smoke. Then came the bombers. Their aim was good and the target small so that the sound of the explosions seemed to mingle into a roll of thunder that went on and on, sending up a great pall of smoke that the wind seized and blew out in a thinning mass over the sea.

Meanwhile the fighters were scrambled for another of the 417 sorties that were flown that fateful day, not only the Poles but also No. 229 Squadron likewise from Northolt, and there was help from the neighbouring Hurricanes from No. 10 Group's base at Middle Wallop. Three of the enemy were accounted for: two of them were bombers, one managing to limp back to France, but the other crashed in the sea off the Isle of Wight while the vanquished Messerschmitt fell on the island. At the Supermarine works only three Spitfires were destroyed, although many that were standing semi-complete had to be repaired. There is no question, however, that the raid had been a success and apart from the casualties, amounting to almost forty this time, the works, at that time the chief production centre for the Supermarine fighters, was severely damaged so that plans to disperse production which were already in existence were pressed ahead with greater vigour. London suffered another attack after dark the same night.

There is no doubt that the city on the edge of No. 11 Group's area had suffered a severe mauling. Here in happier times the flying boats including the *Mayo Composite* had been sights in the seaplane berth alongside such proud ocean-going liners as the *Queen Mary*, but the attacks that had taken place were to mark a change of enemy tactics that was in a sense an admission of failure in the daylight assaults which had marked the previous weeks. This seemed to be confirmed on the Friday, not only by another attack on Filton but also by a massive raid at the heart of No. 11's area, London itself.

Rain falling just after dawn was beginning to clear when the first reports were to send the new rash of coloured counters across the Operations Rooms' tables. In the main the attack was aimed at the Kent coast by formations of Messerschmitt 110s with an escort of their single-seat counterparts, although the defenders were a little later puzzled to note a blip on the RDF screens that seemed to indicate another group of enemy aircraft obviously keeping a rendezvous for a coming sortie.

That this was all part of a concerted plan became clearer when the first of the Nazi machines roared over the coast near to Brighton, but seemed to drop their bombs indiscriminately. At much the same time others appeared over the coast of Dover and Dungeness. At the former it had been a common tactic for single-seaters to come in at low level before suddenly rearing up over the cliffs, lob their load at a convenient target and then turn once more seawards dropping for safety below cliff level for the dash home. Now newly installed anti-aircraft guns above the chalk faces that dropped down to the Channel had put an end to this.

Even so raids of like nature were even then being carried out and they were certainly useful in keeping the interceptors that Park had sent off in a state of continuous occupation until fuel and ammunition ran low, although a major attack timed to follow immediately caught the defenders at a serious disadvantage. This was what seemed to be planned on this occasion, the circling machines that had caused some query earlier being, it was now plain, part of an escort for a coming major attack. Meanwhile Dover was under bombardment from the cross-Channel guns and a pair of farm-workers at Deal claimed that they had been machine-gunned while threshing in the open fields, although they had been alerted by the sound of the warnings from the nearby built-up area since the almost continuous alarms that were often ignored had become rare in the previous week.

At this point the circling fighters' movements took on a hopeless air and it was plain that the bombers they had been detailed to protect had missed them. This established, the ball was in Park's court and he played it with skill so that a whole armada was for once ready to meet the attackers, including Nos 19 and 41 Squadron's Spitfires. These were able to concentrate on the bombers instead of tackling the Messerschmitts as was their usual duty, leaving the slower machines to the rugged Hurricanes.

As midday approached it was clear to the enemy that their tactics had on this occasion failed, and as a result the Luftwaffe formations were detailed to attack a pair of simultaneous targets to split the defence. The greater part of these formations, flying in great stepped-up groups with the unsynchronized beat of their motors seeming to fill the air with sound, was directed against London, although a few in fact were to penetrate far beyond Redhill and Reigate in Surrey. To meet this early afternoon attack 229 and 303 Squadrons were put into the air in company with No. 1 (Canadian) Squadron. Flung as they were against the unsuspecting crews of the Junkers 88s, the defenders had the advantage and it was not long before the black-cross machines were seen to be turning away and loosing their bombs at whatever targets presented themselves to the fleeing formations so that on this occasion it was only a persistent token force that managed to fight its way through to drop their bombs on the capital.

The following day saw something of a repeat of the activities of the Friday, and in Dover the public warning coincided with the peak of the Saturday shopping activity. By now, however, a complete reversal of the earlier state of affairs had taken place and alerts were so frequent that it was impossible for all normal activities to cease, so that workers in the shops continued to serve customers in the normal way. At the same time attacks were delivered once more in the vicinity of the Isle of Wight but the cost to the defenders was high. Fifteen of their number were brought down, six of the pilots being saved at a cost of four machines to the enemy, totals made the more disappointing by the fact that the whole of the 11 Group fighter force was thrown against the enemy, which was showing evidence of new tactics, the frequent change of these being in itself an indication that the Nazi plans had gone awry. The new measures consisted of using smaller formations made up in the main of the relatively faster Junkers 88 which were protected by vast numbers of Messerschmitt 109s, all of them flying fairly high to place the defenders at the disadvantage of having to take sufficient time to gain altitude.

In addition to this there were other signs that all was not well in the Luftwaffe's camp, for the type of targets that were now being picked were almost all of an industrial nature, the destruction of which would be of no immediate advantage to the anticipated invasion forces. The fact is that since the 17th of the month the invasion had been cancelled, at least temporarily, a fact unknown in London, although it was recognized that the break-up of the weather would soon reduce the chances of a successful seaborne operation being carried out. Although there were fighter sweeps against London on the last day of the month, mounted during the morning and again in the afternoon, when a widely flung battle developed over Kent, the invasion barges that Bomber Command were still pounding in the French ports would clearly not be needed as a result of the new air action. On this day too there was even scope for some offensive RAF work within sight of home waters for, in company with fire from the Dover long-range batteries, bombers' tracks blossomed on the plotting tables as they flew out to deal with an enemy convoy in the English Channel.

A once-popular claim that the Battle of Britain ended on 5th October is now less frequently heard. Certain it is that there was no dramatic end or even reduction of enemy activity on that day, when targets in Kent and South-ampton were attacked. The anti-aircraft defences typified by the 75th (Cinque Ports) Heavy AA Regiment which defended Dover continued to toil at their guns, although the targets were now in that area more often lone raiders and it was one of these which on that day dropped several bombs on the battered Kent coast town. Most of these fell harmlessly into the sea but one fell on a wing of the Officers' Mess at Connaught Barracks. Two days later Dover again suffered in the early morning when four bombs fell in the St James Street area, already hard hit. The three fatalities all died later in hospital, the first being a 61-year-old man, Mr Benjamin Botten. At noon there was a similar occurrence when a bomb fell on *Burke*, a trawler earmarked for mine sweeping which was at the time undergoing repairs by the Bulwark Engineering Company in Granville Dock.

If, apart from the night bombing which was part of an entirely different campaign, it seemed that No. 11 Group's Battle of Britain was to end with a whimper rather than a bang, those who believed as much were proved wrong on Tuesday 29th October when a resumption of intense air activity was so fierce that it seemed to mark the beginning of a fresh series of daylight assaults. It was fairly late in the morning when the first important attack developed at about 11 a.m. The raiders were entirely Messerschmitt 109Es, some with single bombs under their bellies and these were engaged by Park's fighters high over Deal and Dover so that the contrails that had marked the summer's fighting were obscured by the haze. The RAF having been drawn irre-trievably into the mêlée, the bomb-carriers found little difficulty in bypassing the defenders and making for London, where they released their loads near to Charing Cross railway station, no doubt aiming for the bridge there.

The normal fighters having done their diversionary work well they withdrew leaving the 11 Group aircraft to prepare for the next anticipated attack; this was not long in coming half an hour after noon, being mounted in part by

Jagdbombern I and II Gruppen of Lehrgeschwader 2 escorted by the First and Second Gruppen of JG51, in the company of 3/Erprobungsgruppe 210 flying their own Jagdbombern, which like the remainder of the aircraft were Messerschmitt 109Es, those of the Jabos being Me109E-4/B and E-7 variants.

To counter these Keith Park had detailed No. 222 Squadron's Spitfires to deliver a rear attack timed to coincide with those from Tangmere's Westhampnett-based 602 Squadron diving from above where they had been waiting at 28,000 feet. Meanwhile the Hurricanes of 615 and 229 Squadrons, the latter operating from dispersal at Fairey Aviation's Heathrow airfield, to which a posting meant lodging in much-envied "civvy" digs.

Completely outmanoeuvred on this occasion the Nazi force fled with the Hurricanes of No. 602 in pursuit, bringing down four of the raiders during the chase, although Samson in his diary records one of them being a Junkers 88, indicating either an error of reporting or the encounter with a raider from another returning sortie over the Channel.

As time passed it was obvious that at first No. 11 Group and then the neighbouring areas had a new problem on their hands, that of night interception as the daylight fighting slowly faded. In the new set of circumstances the strife was just as impersonal as it had been in the earlier engagements so that both service personnel and civilians alike spoke of the enemy both collectively and individually as "they" or "he". Just occasionally, however, a few people had the disquieting thought that among individual flyers from the other side the term "German" might not be synonymous with "Nazi", as some branches of the news media seemed to make out. Just such a query was presented to Mr Fry, the man who had witnessed the destruction of the Junkers 88 over his farm in August, and he recalls it thus:

As was usual in those days, we had poultry on range, which meant shutting them up at night and I had just finished doing so when I heard what I took to be a bomber in the distance; I stopped and leant up against one of the houses listening to see if it was one of "ours" or "theirs" and sure enough it had the familiar sound of an enemy machine.

Now behind this I could pick out the lighter sound of what appeared to be a fighter. As I stood there listening there were suddenly two bursts of cannon fire distinguished by the heavier note and slower rate of fire: there were just two bursts which set me thinking that there should be some empty cartridge cases flying about so it seemed that now was the time to get under cover, as being hit on the head by a 50-mm cannon case wouldn't do one much good, but before I had a chance to do anything, both engines of the bomber cut out—dead, and I thought, "Gosh, he's been hit, he'll unload his bombs", so I really started looking for a ditch.

Now I could hear him starting to whine down, so I jumped into the nearest ditch and buried my head in the dirt. Suddenly there was a mighty "crump" followed by silence and I took this to be a signal that the machine had gone over making it safe to look up. I did so and there caught in a couple of searchlight beams were two parachutes opening, so I dashed indoors for my Home Guard forage cap and by this time we had some rifles, so now properly fitted out I made my way down to the Guard House.

On the way I could see the glow from the bomber that had burst into flames after it had crashed, a few hundred yards away, and then quite suddenly the whole thing blew up in a veritable "Brock's Benefit" with Very lights, flares etc. making it quite a sight.

I reported to the Guard Room and our sergeant said, "We've captured one of the crew, two of them are dead and there's another somewhere around. You, Fry, and Reynolds (he was a groom from one of the local stables and measured about four foot nothing) go off on patrol and see if you can find the missing man." So with another chap we set off in our old 1928 Austin Twelve.

On the second trip, suddenly in the middle of the road we saw this white figure of a man in a Sidcot-type suit. "Golly, parachutists," one of us yelled and we all piled out while the figure stood in the middle of the road with his hands up. We frisked him to make sure he didn't have any weapons and our next problem was to get him back to the Guard Room. This was solved by Tommy Reynolds who as Corporal in charge told me to follow on in the car while the other two marched ahead with the captive.

Now this German could speak a little English and he asked if any of his comrades had been killed, and we told him that two bodies had been found. At this he sat down on the verge and the big man, he was fully six feet two, began to sob, muttering to himself in his misery.

For a moment I felt quite sorry for him but there was nothing for it but to remember the reason for his coming to England and so with me following in the Austin, Tommy Reynolds sloped arms and marching beside the big German who was limping a little, we brought our prisoner home.

Incidents like this were typical of the long hard summer that had gone. The eagle of the Luftwaffe had ended its days of hoped-for triumph and the first victory against the Nazis had been scored; afterwards the proud bird must hunt in the dark.

CHAPTER THIRTEEN

. . . and afterwards

At Hornchurch, Pilot Officer Stephen of No. 74 Squadron found it almost impossible to avert his gaze from the western sky. Beyond lay Northolt and then Hillingdon but from ground level there was now a great wall of lurid light painting the clouds with a glow that had not hung over the capital since the Great Fire in the days of Charles II. As a Londoner he felt frustrated and horrified for there seemed so little that could be done. The bombers had left for some time now but the legacy of their visit was to last for many hours as great storms of flame swept through the East End speeded by the artificial winds of their own creation.

From the air the picture was even more awe-inspiring as the skeletal shapes of buildings could be clearly made out, dark against the background of fire after the first mass raid by the Luftwaffe. Occasionally the yellow glow with its multitude of ruddy hearts would change in hue and an explosion of almost white light would bathe the panorama beneath before slowly subsiding, as staunch Victorian warehouses suddenly buckled and collapsed, sending firemen who had been watching the tell-tale piles of rubble mount up as indicators to danger level rushing for what cover they could find.

Yet within this nightmare spectacle there was, unrecognized, an indication of victory for the defenders of No. 11 Group, for what had been the Battle of Britain was becoming the Blitz, as the aftermath was soon called, shortening to a comfortable and almost English word Hitler's boast of Blitzkrieg—Lightning War.

There was no sudden end to the greatest air battle of all time, no sharp cessation marked by victory bells. It ended as it had begun, a slow merging from one type of activity to another; and just as the tracery of death like the white contrails patterned in the summer sky was to remain for ever in the minds of some the imprint of the daylight fighting, so the smell of burnt wood in the air haunts for ever the nostrils of others as the evocation of the night bombing. By the standards that were established later the high-explosive bombs used in the main were of small capacity, being largely 50 kilos in weight, but these were dropped often in concert with "Parachute Mines". These had a far greater blast potential and a thin casing but were not very accurate. It was one of these, identified by the coarse material of its canopy, not the traditional silk, with its half-inch thick, plaited green lines, no doubt of cotton, that had one night come to rest without exploding with the canopy draped over a corner of the building directly over No. 11 Group's Operations Room, a danger heightened when orders to clear the transport yard had brought every vehicle trundling past setting up vibrations which might at any moment have detonated it!

The greater part of the damage was the result of dropping thousands of thermite incendiaries together with oil bombs, a fire-raising device combining fuel oil and phosphorus. One of the earliest incidents of the Blitz is recalled by John Garwood, who was in the St George Tavern near Dragon Road in south-east London when one of these devices dropped nearby.

Our pub was not more than two or three blocks away and at the same time ordinary incendiaries dropped on the roof there one night. I had already got myself a souvenir of the oil bomb round the corner in the form of a bit of twisted metal but my main memory of a few moments later is toiling away at a stirrup pump to damp down the rafters.

The spirit of the nation was quite different now even if so short a time ago such aircraft as Tiger Moth and Miles Magister trainers had been fitted up as light bombers to be used on what would have proved suicide missions against invading troops. The atmosphere was now one of dogged determination and there was every belief that an invasion was still likely, perhaps the following spring. There was therefore less for the Pioneers to do immediately. In some cases they had assisted in ranging out the line upon line of derelict cars on open areas of land that seemed to offer potential landing grouds for troop gliders and their motor coach companies, transported in civilian buses hastily painted khaki, had toured the country erecting double-apron fences with triple Dennet wiring, digging slit trenches at crossroads to act as sand-bagged machine-gun posts and excavating anti-tank ditches, perhaps alongside the strange cylindrical smoke-screen producers that had sprung up on the roadsides. Mines too were laid, sometimes in conjunction with "dragons' teeth", concrete pyramids ranged across even town roads sometimes to leave marks that may still be picked out today, so many decades later.

The fact that emerged from the transition from daylight to night bombing is that the Nazi air arm had been forced to admit defeat and suddenly so. Already there was a likelihood that had the raids of July opened with concentrated attacks on airfields the outcome might have been different. This is in no way to diminish the success of Dowding, Park and their "chicks", as Winston Churchill had called the fighter pilots, yet there was in the Luftwaffe a feeling among some that they had not been supported as they deserved. Among modern historians too it has frequently been claimed that Fighter Command was stronger at the end of the battle than at its beginning. Like so many trite observations this is true only as far as it goes. Certainly the figures reveal that at the beginning of the period spanning mid-July to the end of October 550 fighters were available, compared to a total of some 700 (including about 170 night fighters) in the later periods. However, this, although it makes a good showing when compared with the sum of about 250 operational fighters with a 75 per cent service-ability in the mid-battle period, takes no account of the fact that the total of *experienced* fighter pilots had seriously diminished.

Indeed the position of Fighter Command after the battle and the fact that the enemy was in a position to continue attacks on this country, albeit during the hours of darkness, have caused some commentators to doubt if there was any victory during the summer of 1940 at all. It has further been voiced that there never was any danger of these islands being invaded as the strength of the Royal Navy and its control of the Channel would have prevented any seaborne invasion troops being put ashore.

The submission of arguments such as these seem to indicate a gross ignorance of tactical matters, for to regard the campaign of night bombing as a mere continuance of the summer's battles does not take into consideration that the Blitz was the opening of a new policy, namely the one of attempting to gain victory by first wearing down the civilian population instead of attacking targets that had some sort of military or strategic potential, as had been done in the various phases of the Battle of Britain when No. 11 Group had suffered the brunt of these.

Further, the contention also assumes somewhat naïvely that with the RAF beaten out of the air the Royal Navy would have survived sufficiently long as a protector of the narrow seas to frustrate ultimately the attempts of a determined and vicious enemy with his morale at its zenith after the unbroken series of successes in France and the Low Countries. Both the preliminary attacks which resulted in the loss of Singapore and Crete prove that this is untrue. The similarities between these situations and that prevailing in 1940 were very great, for sea power failed to save the day on either occasion once command of the air was lost.

In addition to this it has become fashionable to state that the victory against the daylight attacks of the Luftwaffe was achieved because the defenders were flying from their own airfields and were therefore always conscious of what they were defending in recognizable terms: not a vague ideal perhaps dreamed up by ambitious politicians and constantly repeated in theatrical terms for which many fighting men are supposed to be prepared to die for, but the everyday things to which those defenders had become accustomed throughout their lives. In short this belief has been summed up in the comfortable statement that "the home team always wins".

An argument such as this is not only wildly short of the truth and tarnishes the lustre of the victory by "the Few", it is also dangerous in the extreme since it seems to state by implication that in the last analysis short commons with regard to equipment, poor organization and indiscipline are all compensated for when the "home team" is fielded. In fact it is amply shown that defenders even of their native soil are in as hopeless a situation as any when these three evils burden them, and the Second World War gave several illustrations of this.

The seeds of victory tor No. 11 Group in particular and Fighter Command in general were sown well before, in the days that saw the last age before family life collapsed and with it the tenets of order, organization, allegiance, loyalty and obedience that went with it. These were also echoed in the educational system of the day, so that "slovenly" was a shameful word, be it applied to thought or deed, which had not yet been softened and replaced by today's equivalent term, "casual". Wellington is (quite incorrectly) quoted as having claimed that the Battle of Waterloo was won on the playing fields of Eton, but it would be wrong to assume that the victory of 1940 began somewhere similar, for the day when the fighting man had more brawn than brain had vanished even then. Nevertheless, it would seem that the origins of victory lay deep in the homes, schools and general attitude to life of the preceding days.

More than four decades after, it is interesting to examine just what type of men it was who drove themselves on against the onslaught. From whence had they come, the pilots who daily waited at dispersal white-faced with weariness yet flew with exact precision in formation still? A high proportion were professional flyers or volunteers since they would all have taken flying training at least a year before. These latter came into the RAF via a number of schemes that existed in the late 1930s which were all devised to form a reserve of trained men, the Volunteer Reserve scheme and the county-orientated Auxiliary Air Force being the foremost of these.

Yet when it came to the inevitable conclusion all these, no matter from what background they came, or what calling they had followed, were as one in the service; rank set up no barriers and nor did experience of things past, so that when No. 610 Squadron was resting after a severe mauling in the south, the newly joined Sergeant Ward-Smith, one of those drafted in as part of a reconstituted squadron that would be second to none, found that there was no side, no attitudes struck, no lofty superiority assumed by the more experienced. Officers, sergeants, all were just *pilots* who flew together, drank together and played together, some inevitably dying together when the recall to the fray was answered.

None of these men would have been aware that they

were making a piece of history, whether they were aircrew or the tradesmen among whom discipline was never enforced on duty, the comparatively forgotten men who have not been invested by time with any of the qualities of knights in shining armour but were as indispensable to the final victory as a match is to a conflagration. The only atmosphere was of men just doing their job. Their trade was killing and like any others who plied it in the air they were to their own way of thinking just another lot of military flyers who were doing what an air force existed for.

As a consequence of this only among a very few British was there any animosity towards the enemy. There was no killer instinct, no "bloody Hun" attitude: these were the products of the earth-bound reporter and occasionally there was real respect for the poor devil in the cross-marked target. There was a case, rare but not isolated, when watchers on the ground stilled their cheers as a Messerschmitt was seen to go down after a particularly gallant single combat, and from the sun came a Spitfire, almost leisurely in its descent. The pilot circled the spot where a widening circle of foam in the Channel marked the grave of his adversary before dipping his wings in salute and climbing away. But generally air fighting was completely impersonal. It was just a job to destroy aeroplanes with black crosses on them, and if you did not, then the other brought you down.

It has frequently been said that no one at the time knew the summer's aerial engagements as the Battle of Britain, but this is untrue. The name was given by Winston Churchill in an evening broadcast a full fortnight after the last soldier had been plucked from the northern French beaches, for what General Weygand was to call the Battle of France dragged on for a couple of weeks. It was when announcing that this was at long last over that Churchill added, "I expect that the Battle of Britain is about to begin." The words caught the spirit of the time and were reflected in the newspapers the following morning, the *Daily Sketch* on

Wednesday 19th June declaring in its headline, "Battle of Britain: R.A.F. On Offensive." Words which were to become part of history had been spoken.

The month that followed was used by both sides to prepare, the Luftwaffe being able to use three airfleets, the most important being Luftflotten 2 and 3 based in Belgium and Holland, and France respectively, with a grand total of 2,500 aircraft consisting in round figures of 1,130 bombers and 320 Stukas. To this must be added 1,050 fighters, 800 of them being single-seaters, which meant the Messerschmitt 109E, for the Heinkel 113 (the publicity title for the officially designated He 100D, thus avoiding the "unlucky" number) was never used in the fight despite its occasional appearance in RAF combat reports.

Yet despite the assembly of such a vast aerial armada (Luftflotte 5 was based in Norway and Denmark and therefore not flung against No. 11 Group) it is surprisingly argued today that there was never any real intention of invading these shores. What such a stance does not explain is why the airfleets were assembled, in the light of the fact that no war could ever be won exclusively by offensive air power? Allied to this must be the fact that although Hitler lacked personal ability as a strategic commander, both he and his High Command were nothing if not gifted opportunists and once the Fighter Command of the RAF had been brought to its knees the climate would have been ideal for an invasion force to cross the Channel and subdue England. It is perfectly possible for an air force to be eliminated from the air alone and without physical occupation by enemy troops, as is shown by reference to the events in northern France in 1944 when the Luftwaffe was driven from the air, as the Egyptian Air Force was destroyed by the strikes of more recent years when the Israelis staged a pre-emptive onslaught against their neighbours.

What is not realized in any appreciable measure, even at this distance in time, is that the victory which Keith Park and his no less gifted superior, Dowding, and assistant,

Gibbs, achieved was far more than the salvation of the British way of life. With the whole of Europe and Scandinavia under the Nazi yoke, Soviet Russia kept quiet, the Nazis believed, with a Treaty of Friendship, and Great Britain occupied, there is every likelihood that the next glance of greed that Hitler would have made with covetous eyes would have been across the Atlantic. Not for nothing did Churchill choose to say on the historic eve of battle, "We have become the sole champions, now in arms to defend the world cause."

APPENDIX

Fighter Squadron Bases and Movements, 1940

In order to present a complete picture of the fighter squadron situation those operating outside No. 11 Group are included, bases within the area of the group being indicated in italics. Detachments are ignored. It should also be borne in mind that some squadrons had been operating from bases in France during the first part of June or else flying to cover the Dunkirk evacuation.

Sqdn No.	June	July	August	September
1	*Tangmere* from 23.6	*Tangmere*	*Tangmere* to *Northolt*	*Northolt*
3	*Wick*	*Wick*	*Wick*	*Wick* to *Castletown*
17	*Debden*	*Debden*	*Debden* to *Tangmere*	*Tangmere* to *Debden*
19	Fowlmere	Fowlmere to Duxford to Fowlmere	Fowlmere	Fowlmere

Sqdn No.	June	July	August	September
23	Collyweston	Collyweston	Collyweston to Wittering	Wittering
25	Martlesham Heath	Martlesham Heath	Martlesham Heath	Martlesham Heath to North Weald
29	Debden to Digby	Digby	Digby	Digby
32	Biggin Hill	Biggin Hill	Biggin Hill to Acklington	Acklington
41	Catterick to Hornchurch	Hornchurch	Hornchurch to Catterick	Catterick to Hornchurch
43	Tangmere	Tangmere to North Weald	Northolt to Tangmere	Tangmere to Usworth
54	Hornchurch to Rochford	Rochford to Hornchurch to Catterick	Catterick to Hornchurch	Hornchurch to Catterick
56	North Weald	North Weald	North Weald	North Weald to Boscombe Down
64	Kenley	Kenley	Kenley to Leconfield	Leconfield
65	Hornchurch	Hornchurch	Hornchurch to Turnhouse	Turnhouse
66	Coltishall	Coltishall	Coltishall to Kenley	Kenley to Gravesend
71				Church Fenton from 19.9
72	Gravesend to Acklington	Acklington	Acklington to Biggin Hill	Biggin Hill to Croydon to Biggin Hill
73	Church Fenton	Church Fenton	Church Fenton	Church Fenton to Castle Camps
74	Leconfield to Rochford	Rochford to Hornchurch	Hornchurch to Wittering to Kirton-in-Lindsey	Kirton-in-Lindsey to Coltishall
79	Digby to Biggin Hill	Biggin Hill to Hawkinge to Sealand to Acklington	Acklington to Biggin Hill	Biggin Hill to Pembrey
85	Debden to Martlesham Heath	Martlesham Heath	Martlesham Heath to Debden to Croydon	Croydon to Castle Camps to Church Fenton
87	Church Fenton	Church Fenton	Church Fenton	Church Fenton
92	Northolt to Hornchurch to Pembrey	Pembrey	Pembrey	Pembrey to Biggin Hill
111	Croydon	Croydon	Croydon to Debden	Debden to Croydon to Drem

Sqdn No.	June	July	August	September
141	Turnhouse to *West Malling*	*West Malling* to Grangemouth	Grangemouth to Dyce to Turnhouse	Turnhouse to Drem
145	*Tangmere*	*Tangmere* to Westhampnett	Westhampnett to Drem	Drem
151	*Martlesham Heath*	*Martlesham Heath*	*Martlesham Heath* to Stapleford	Stapleford to Digby
152	Acklington	Acklington to Warmwell	Warmwell	Warmwell
213	*Biggin Hill* to Wittering to *Biggin Hill* to Exeter	Exeter	Exeter	Exeter to *Tangmere*
219	Catterick	Catterick	Catterick	Catterick
222	*Hornchurch*	*Hornchurch*	*Hornchurch*	*Hornchurch*
229	Wittering	Wittering	Wittering	Wittering to *Northolt*
232		Sumburgh to Castletown	Castletown	Castletown
234	Church Fenton to St Eval	St Eval	St Eval to Middle Wallop	Middle Wallop to St Eval
238	*Tangmere* to Middle Wallop	Middle Wallop	Middle Wallop	Middle Wallop to St Eval
242	Coltishall	Coltishall	Coltishall	Coltishall
245	Drem to Turnhouse	Turnhouse to Aldergrove	Aldergrove	Aldergrove
247			Roborough	Roborough
249	Leconfield	Leconfield to Church Fenton	Church Fenton to Boscombe Down	Boscombe Down to *North Weald*
253	Kirton-in-Lindsey	Kirton-in-Lindsey to Turnhouse	Turnhouse to Prestwick to *Kenley*	*Kenley*
257	*Hendon*	*Hendon* to *Northolt*	*Northolt* to *Debden*	*Debden* to *Martlesham Heath*
263	Drem to Grangemouth	Grangemouth	Grangemouth	Grangemouth to Drem
264	Duxford	Duxford to Fowlmere to Kirton-in-Lindsey	Kirton-in-Lindsey to *Hornchurch* to Kirton-in-Lindsey	Kirton-in-Lindsey
266	Wittering	Wittering	Wittering to *Eastchurch* to *Hornchurch* to Wittering	Wittering to *Martlesham Heath*
302		Leconfield	Leconfield	Leconfield
303			*Northolt*	*Northolt*

Sqdn No.	June	July	August	September
306			Church Fenton	Church Fenton
307				Kirton-in-Lindsey
310		Duxford	Duxford	Duxford
312			Duxford	Duxford to Speke
401	Middle Wallop	Middle Wallop to Croydon	*Croydon* to Northolt	*Northolt*
501	*Croydon*	*Croydon* to Middle Wallop to Gravesend	*Gravesend* to Kenley	*Kenley*
504	Wick to Castletown	Castletown	Castletown	Castletown to Catterick to *Hendon* to Filton
600	*Northolt*	*Northolt* to Manston	*Manston* to Hornchurch	*Hornchurch* to *Redhill* to Catterick
601	*Tangmere* to Middle Wallop to *Tangmere*	*Tangmere*	*Tangmere* to Debden	*Debden*
602	Drem	Drem	Drem to Westhampnett	Westhampnett
603	Dyce	Dyce	Dyce to Montrose to Hornchurch	*Hornchurch*
604	*Manston* to Northolt	*Northolt* to Gravesend to Middle Wallop	Middle Wallop to Warmwell to Middle Wallop	Middle Wallop
605	Drem	Drem	Drem	Drem to *Croydon*
607	Usworth to *Tangmere*	*Tangmere*	*Tangmere*	*Tangmere*
609	*Northolt*	*Northolt* to Middle Wallop	Middle Wallop	Middle Wallop
610	*Gravesend*	*Gravesend* to Biggin Hill	*Biggin Hill* to Acklington	Acklington
611	Digby	Digby to Tern Hill	Tern Hill to Digby	Tern Hill
615	*Kenley*	*Kenley*	*Kenley* to Prestwick	Prestwick
616	*Rochford* to Leconfield	Leconfield	Leconfield to *Kenley*	*Kenley* to Coltishall to Kirton-in-Lindsey

Index

222 *Index*